THE
100
PRAYERS
of the Bible

ED STRAUSS

BARBOUR BOOKS
An Imprint of Barbour Publishing, Inc.

Print ISBN 978-1-63409-631-7

eBook Editions:
Adobe Digital Edition (.epub) 978-1-63409-633-1
Kindle and MobiPocket Edition (.prc) 978-1-63409-632-4

Cover Photograph: Eric Enstrom, Wikimedia

Published by Barbour Books, an imprint of Barbour Publishing, Inc., P.O. Box 719, Uhrichsville, Ohio 44683, www.barbourbooks.com

Our mission is to publish and distribute inspirational products offering exceptional value and biblical encouragement to the masses.

Member of the
Evangelical Christian
Publishers Association

Printed in the United States of America.

Contents

INTRODUCTION

This book, just as the title says, contains the top one hundred prayers of the Bible. You may be surprised by their diversity—from agonized requests, demands, protests, and complaints to pleas for mercy, shouts of praise, and benedictions—but all are heartfelt cries to God.

These prayers also deal with a wide spectrum of situations. People's messy lives, then as now, sparked desperation for divine intervention. They experienced complex personal problems, weariness and frustration, pressing financial needs, life-threatening illnesses. They needed specific guidance, and were given nearly unbelievable promises. Whatever their situation, they were forced to look to God to do a miracle.

It's our hope that meditating on how men and women of old implored God in times of need, and how He acted in their lives, will inspire you to believe that He cares for you and hears *your* prayers today as well. He's still the same all-powerful, compassionate God now as He was then. He says, "I am the LORD, I change not" (Malachi 3:6 KJV). And "Jesus Christ is the same yesterday and today and forever" (Hebrews 13:8 NIV).

Are you frustrated and at your wit's end? Are you facing a problem that is much bigger than you're able to handle? Somewhere, sometime, someone in the Bible faced a similar situation, turned to God in prayer, and expected Him to answer—and He did.

No matter how desperate your situation, how deep your sorrow, how acute your need, God is present to help. He may not answer every one of your prayers the way you think He should or in the exact time frame you wish Him to, but if you believe and persevere, He will answer.

1. Prayer beneath the Stars

One evening when the star-crowded heavens unfurled above the dark land of Canaan, the Lord gave Abraham (then called Abram) a vision. God's voice impressed itself on his senses, saying, "Do not be afraid, Abram. I am your shield, your very great reward" (Genesis 15:1 NIV). Abraham knew that God was real and that he was in the presence of his all-powerful Creator, so he took the opportunity to pour out the deepest need of his heart.

He prayed, "Sovereign LORD, what can you give me since I remain childless and the one who will inherit my estate is Eliezer of Damascus?" (Genesis 15:2 NIV). Abraham's heart was so heavy that he repeated himself: "You have given me no children; so a servant in my household will be my heir" (Genesis 15:3 NIV).

But God answered, "This man will not be your heir, but a son who is your own flesh and blood will be your heir" (Genesis 15:4 NIV). Abraham then felt God leading him out of his tent. As he stepped outside, the Lord said, "Look up at the sky and count the stars—if indeed you can count them" (Genesis 15:5 NIV). Abraham was overwhelmed with the impossibility of the task. There were far, far too many to count. Then God said, "So shall your offspring be" (Genesis 15:5 NIV).

"Abraham believed the LORD, and [God] credited it to him as righteousness" (Genesis 15:6 NIV).

Abraham's faith in God's promise not only made him righteous in God's eyes, but it ensured that his request would be granted. Sure enough, some years later, his wife, Sarah, became pregnant and gave birth to a son, Isaac (Genesis 21:1–2). Even though it took a long time, Abraham "staggered not at the promise of God through unbelief; but was strong in faith" (Romans 4:20 KJV).

Abraham's prayers sprang from his deep relationship with God. Note that the Lord began by telling Abraham that He Himself was Abraham's greatest reward. He finished that night's encounter by declaring Abraham righteous in His sight.

Abraham loved and worshiped God before anything else, so God was pleased to grant his request. "Delight yourself also in the LORD, and He shall give you the desires of your heart" (Psalm 37:4 NKJV). "Seek first the kingdom of God and His righteousness, and all these things shall be added to you" (Matthew 6:33 NKJV).

2. Requesting Clarification

Often, even though you believe that God has promised to do something for you, you want to be doubly sure. You may have received the distinct impression that He would be with you and bless you in an endeavor, but you also know you could be mistaken. You might have misunderstood what God intended. And though you claim promises from His Word, you don't want to be presumptuous. So you ask for clarification and confirmation. This is perfectly scriptural.

When Abraham first arrived in Canaan, God promised, "To your descendants I will give this land" (Genesis 12:7 NKJV). A couple of years later, He said, "All the land which you see I give to you and your descendants forever" (Genesis 13:15 NKJV). After a few more years, God said, "I am the LORD, who brought you out of Ur. . .to give you this land to inherit it" (Genesis 15:7 NKJV).

God had made the same promise on three occasions. But Abraham asked, "Lord GOD, how shall I know that I will inherit it?" (Genesis 15:8 NKJV). You might want to blurt out, "Because God *said* so!" But Abraham wasn't doubting. He just needed clarification. God had promised to give the land "to your descendants," then promised "to give you this land." So Abraham wondered if *he* personally would inherit the land and pass it on to his children. If so, something major needed to happen—and soon. After all, he wasn't getting any younger.

God then clarified *exactly* what He meant. He stated that Abraham would die and be buried without taking possession of the land, but that after four hundred years his descendants would return from another country and inherit Canaan (Genesis 15:13, 15).

God then instructed Abraham to sacrifice animals and cut

them in half. Then, in the darkness, Abraham "saw a smoking firepot and a flaming torch pass between the halves of the carcasses" (Genesis 15:17 NLT). This flaming firepot and torch represented God Himself. And in those days when someone walked between pieces of a sacrifice, they were invoking a curse on themselves, saying, "May I likewise be hewn in two if I don't keep my promise."

In so doing, God was irrevocably binding Himself with a solemn covenant to give the land to Abraham's descendants. And He did.

Asking God for clarification and confirmation is wise.

3. When God Says No

Years passed and Sarah never had a child. Realizing that she was now past the age of childbearing, she gave Abraham her slave girl, Hagar, as a concubine. According to the customs of the day, a child born to a slave could be counted as a child of the legal wife—so, with a little "help" God's promise would be fulfilled. Sure enough, Hagar became pregnant and gave birth to a son whom she named Ishmael.

Thirteen years later Abraham considered the issue of his heir settled. Then one day God told him, "As for Sarai your wife. . . Sarah shall be her name. I will bless her, and indeed I will give you a son by her. Then I will bless her, and she shall be a mother of nations" (Genesis 17:15–16 NASB).

What was Abraham's reaction? He was so startled that he fell to the ground laughing. Sarah was now ninety! How could she bear a child? Abraham knew he was hearing from God, not his imagination, and he didn't mean to be disrespectful, but *this. . .* this was *too funny.*

After Abraham regained control of himself, he got up from the dust and continued praying. He'd been certain that Ishmael was his heir. He'd never considered anyone else. So he prayed, "Oh that Ishmael might live before You!" (Genesis 17:18 NASB). In other words, "But God, I already have a son. Let Ishmael inherit the promises."

God said, "No, but Sarah your wife will bear you a son, and you shall call his name Isaac [Laughter]; and I will establish My covenant with him. . .As for Ishmael [God hears], I have heard you; behold, I will bless him, and will make him fruitful and will multiply him exceedingly. . . . But My covenant I will establish with Isaac" (Genesis 17:19–21 NASB).

God knew that Abraham loved Ishmael, so God blessed him mightily. But He couldn't grant Abraham's request. Ishmael was not the heir. God had a different plan, one that required Abraham to believe in the impossible.

Sometimes God withholds something good from us because He has something better in mind.

4. Boldly Interceding

One day the Lord came to Abraham's camp under the oaks of Mamre, accompanied by two angels. They arrived in the form of mortals. As they were leaving, God informed Abraham that He was about to destroy the wicked cities of the plain because the outcry against Sodom and Gomorrah was great (Genesis 18:20). Now, Abraham's nephew Lot and family lived in Sodom, so Abraham was alarmed.

God had said that the outcry against them was great. Who had been crying out against them if not their victims, living in the same city? Surely, Abraham reasoned, they didn't deserve to be destroyed with their evil oppressors. So he prayed, "Wilt thou also destroy the righteous with the wicked? . . . Shall not the Judge of all the earth do right?" (Genesis 18:23, 25 KJV).

It was a bold approach and Abraham knew it. But he didn't know what else to say. And God relented. He said that if there were fifty righteous people in Sodom, He'd spare the city. Abraham then asked God to spare Sodom if there were only forty-five righteous people there. God agreed. But Abraham still had no peace. So he asked God not to destroy it if it contained only forty godly people. Again, God agreed.

Abraham worried that he was pestering the Lord, but boldly went on to ask Him to spare the city for the sake of thirty, then twenty, then ten people. God agreed each time. The next day, as he watched the thick, black smoke churning skyward, Abraham realized that Sodom had been given over entirely to evil.

Nevertheless, Abraham is a tremendous example of intercession. He was moved with compassion and concern and persevered in praying for others. He boldly appealed to God's sense of justice and mercy. Often we're afraid to pray like that.

We worry that He will get angry if we pester Him too much. We suspect that He will shut us out if we keep on talking. But God literally commands us to not stop praying to Him for others.

The Bible declares, "You who make mention of the LORD, do not keep silent, and give Him no rest till He establishes and till He makes Jerusalem a praise in the earth" (Isaiah 62:6–7 NKJV). Whom or what are you praying for continually?

5. Changing God's Mind?

Many people think that if they pray hard enough, they can change God's mind. They point out that there are scriptures where the Lord declared that He'd do something but a man of God interceded and, so it seems, changed God's will. For example—

God stated that He would destroy Sodom and Gomorrah if they were wicked (Genesis 18:20–21), and after learning that they were, angels urged Lot's family, "Flee for your lives! Don't look back, and don't stop anywhere in the plain! Flee to the mountains or you will be swept away!" (Genesis 19:17 NIV).

Lot protested, "I can't flee to the mountains; this disaster will overtake me, and I'll die. Look, here is a town near enough to run to, and it is small. Let me flee to it." One of the angels replied, "I will grant this request too; I will not overthrow the town you speak of. But flee there quickly" (Genesis 19:19–22 NIV).

Did Lot change God's will? No. God had only sworn to destroy Sodom and Gomorrah. It was always within His will for Zoar to be spared. But if Lot hadn't asked, it too would have been consumed in the conflagration.

In 2 Kings 20:1–5 (NIV), King Hezekiah was sick and wondered if he'd recover. God sent Isaiah with this message: "You are going to die; you will not recover." But when Hezekiah wept and prayed desperately, God sent Isaiah back, saying, "I have heard your prayer and seen your tears; I will heal you." Did Hezekiah change God's mind? No. It was *always* within His will for Hezekiah to be healed. . .but if he hadn't prayed, he would have certainly died.

Again, God threatened to destroy Nineveh, but when its people repented, He didn't destroy it. The reason? God takes no pleasure in the death of the wicked. He longs for the wicked to repent and live (Ezekiel 33:11). He is "a gracious and compassionate God, slow to anger and abounding in love, a God who relents from sending calamity" (Jonah 4:2 NIV).

Let's look at Lot again: he was a "righteous man" (2 Peter 2:7), and James tells us, "The earnest prayer of a righteous person has great power" (James 5:16 NLT). So pray! Your request could be within God's will. But you have to *ask* or it might never happen.

6. Praying for the Right Wife

Isaac was forty years old, so Abraham decided that it was time for him to get married. He summoned his servant, Eliezer, and sent him to Haran in the far north. Abraham was determined that Isaac marry a godly woman from his own people, the Hebrews.

Some time later, Eliezer arrived at a spring outside the town. But how to choose a wife? Picking just *any* woman could prove disastrous! Isaac's wife had to be not only beautiful but virtuous, industrious, and generous. But time was of a premium. Eliezer couldn't spend weeks getting to know the town's women. Besides, a father might claim his daughter was virtuous just to see her married. Eliezer had to depend on God.

He prayed, "O Lord, God of my master, Abraham. . . . Please give me success today, and show unfailing love to my master, Abraham. See, I am standing here beside this spring, and the young women of the town are coming out to draw water. This is my request. I will ask one of them, 'Please give me a drink from your jug.' If she says, 'Yes, have a drink, and I will water your camels, too!'—let her be the one you have selected as Isaac's wife" (Genesis 24:12–14 NLT).

It was an exacting condition. Eliezer had arrived with ten camels. It was highly unlikely that *any* woman would offer to water so many thirsty beasts—for a total stranger, at that. She would have to possess uncommon virtue. But when Rebekah came to the spring, she proved to be just such a woman. When she had fulfilled Eliezer's prayer to the letter, he fell to his knees, overcome with wonder, and praised God. He wasted no time: the next day, Rebekah was riding a camel south to Canaan.

These days, most men and women don't—and shouldn't—depend on a single, spectacular sign to show them whom they should marry. Usually they have ample time to get to know a potential spouse. But God can still grant miraculous signs in response to desperate prayer. There will be times in your personal or business life when you'll be forced to make important decisions and simply won't know what to do.

In such times, just like Eliezer, you must pray and depend on God to make it clear what you are to do.

7. Small Focus, Small Prayers

Jacob had deviously stolen the birthright and the blessing from his brother, and Esau wanted to kill him. So Rebekah persuaded Isaac to send Jacob to Haran "to find a wife." Her real reason was to save him from a dangerous situation.

Isaac now recognized Jacob as his heir, so with his eyes on the big picture, Isaac gave his son this parting blessing: "May God Almighty. . .give you the blessing of Abraham, to you and your descendants with you, that you may inherit the land" (Genesis 28:3–4 NKJV).

As Jacob slept beside the road one night, God appeared and said, "I am the LORD God of Abraham your father and the God of Isaac; the land on which you lie I will give to you and your descendants. . . . Behold, I am with you and will keep you wherever you go, and will bring you back to this land; for I will not leave you until I have done what I have spoken to you" (Genesis 28:13, 15 NKJV).

What promises! God spoke of Jacob's magnificent destiny—a multitude of descendants who would inherit all of Canaan. But Jacob's focus was far smaller: all he could think about was his personal safety, having food, staying warm, and making it back home again. He responded, "If God will be with me, and keep me in this way that I am going, and give me bread to eat and clothing to put on, so that I come back to my father's house in peace, then the LORD shall be my God" (Genesis 28:20–21 NKJV).

God had said that His presence would never leave Jacob. He promised to bless him with descendants who would fill the land. The all-powerful God would certainly keep Jacob alive to ensure this tremendous future happened. That was a given.

But as believers, we can sympathize with Jacob's attitude. Often we, too, get our eyes off God's promises and become anxious. Sometimes all we can think about is how we're going to pay our bills or survive some crisis.

We do well to remember God's promise: " 'For I know the plans I have for you,' declares the LORD, 'plans to prosper you and not to harm you, plans to give you hope and a future' " (Jeremiah 29:11 NIV). Focus on *that* and it will transform your prayer life!

8. Quoting God's Promises

Twenty-one years passed, and Jacob was now headed back to Canaan. With him were his four wives, eleven children, and vast flocks and herds. He sent messengers to inform Esau that he was coming. Better to tell him than for Esau to discover him trying to sneak back into Canaan. But when Jacob's messengers returned, they brought alarming news: Esau was not only riding to meet him, but bringing four hundred armed men!

Jacob was understandably afraid. But his prayer shows his maturity and deepening relationship with God. He was now a spiritual man who looked at his problems in the light of God's promises.

Jacob prayed, "O God of my father Abraham and God of my father Isaac, O LORD, who said to me, 'Return to your country and to your relatives, and I will prosper you,' I am unworthy of all the lovingkindness and of all the faithfulness which You have shown. . . . Deliver me, I pray, from the hand of my brother, from the hand of Esau; for I fear him, that he will come and attack me and the mothers with the children. For You said, 'I will surely prosper you and make your descendants as the sand of the sea, which is too great to be numbered' " (Genesis 32:9–12 NASB).

What a difference in his prayers! Jacob sandwiched his request for protection between two of God's promises—promises that he now quoted. Jacob was declaring, "This is Your Word, Lord. I'm trusting You to fulfill it, and to protect me and mine."

Jacob was afraid, yes, but he reasoned that if God said, "Return to your country and to your relatives, and I will prosper you," that He wasn't sending him back to be killed. Jacob reasoned that for this promise to be fulfilled God had to keep his children safe.

When Esau saw Jacob the next day, "Esau ran to meet him and embraced him, threw his arms around his neck, and kissed him. And they both wept" (Genesis 33:4 NLT). God kept His promise.

9. Prayers of Pain and Confusion

Job experienced terrific misery. God allowed Satan to take away all his possessions, even to kill his sons and daughters. Then Satan "afflicted Job with painful sores from the soles of his feet to the crown of his head" (Job 2:7 NIV). He was in so much pain that he had to sit in a pile of soft ashes.

As his boils filled with pus, Job took a piece of broken pottery and scraped them. Flies laid eggs in the open sores, and soon maggots were crawling all over his body. Job complained, "My body is clothed with worms and scabs, my skin is broken and festering" (Job 7:5 NIV). These sufferings lasted for months.

The pain and discomfort kept him awake at night: "The night drags on, and I toss and turn until dawn" (Job 7:4 NIV). When he finally did fall asleep, he was tormented with nightmares (Job 7:13–15). And he couldn't understand why God was allowing him to suffer so much.

Job's friends assured him that if he confessed his sin, God would restore his health, but Job couldn't think of any sin he had committed. Job did pray about his problems, but mostly he poured out his heart in bitter complaints.

Job cried out to the Lord in his pain and confusion: "Oh, that I might have my request, that God would grant what I hope for, that God would be willing to crush me, to. . .cut off my life!" (Job 6:8–9 NIV). This was a bitter prayer, and Job went on to request: "Turn away from me so I can have a moment's joy before I go to the place of no return" (Job 10:20–21 NIV). God didn't answer these.

But God did answer these prayers: "Grant me these two things, God. . .Withdraw your hand far from me, and stop frightening me with your terrors. Then summon me and. . .show me my offense and my sin" (Job 13:20–23 NIV). God appeared to Job, mercifully brought his suffering to an end, and restored his health and his possessions. "The LORD restored his fortunes and gave him twice as much as he had before" (Job 42:10 NIV).

It's often the same today. God sorts through believers' agonized, confused prayers and brings them answers they never asked for and solutions they couldn't imagine in their darkness.

10. Send Someone Else, Lord

It's often said that prayer is "talking with God." But most people will never engage in conversation with God quite like Moses did. When he approached the burning bush, the Lord began speaking audibly with him. And even though Moses knew he was talking with God Himself, he frequently balked at His commands.

First, Moses protested, "Who am I to appear before Pharaoh? Who am I to lead the people of Israel out of Egypt?" (Exodus 3:11 NLT). Then he questioned, "If I go to the people of Israel and tell them, 'The God of your ancestors has sent me to you,' they will ask me, 'What is his name?' Then what should I tell them?" (Exodus 3:13 NLT). Moses raised more objections: "What if they won't believe me or listen to me? What if they say, 'The LORD never appeared to you'?" (Exodus 4:1 NLT). Each time, God patiently answered Moses' questions.

But then Moses tried getting out of the job altogether. He argued, "O Lord, I'm not very good with words. I never have been, and I'm not now, even though you have spoken to me. I get tongue-tied, and my words get tangled." But God said firmly, "Now go! I will be with you as you speak, and I will instruct you in what to say" (Exodus 4:10, 12 NLT).

Finally, Moses blurted out what he was really thinking: "Lord, please! Send anyone else" (Exodus 4:13 NLT). Then God got mad. But He had anticipated even this, so He told Moses that his brother Aaron was already coming to join him. Aaron would be his spokesperson, but Moses still had the task of leading the Israelites out of Egypt.

Moses didn't hesitate to ask God questions. His questions revealed his lack of self-confidence and unwillingness, true, but they were honest questions, so God answered them.

One of the most important reasons for prayer is to seek God's will, and to yield to it. Yet how often do we try to get out of it and get God to rubber-stamp what we want instead? Better to have Isaiah's attitude. When God asked, "Whom shall I send, and who will go for us?" Isaiah answered, "Here am I; send me" (Isaiah 6:8 KJV).

11. Nobody Listens to Me!

When Moses first returned to Egypt, the Israelites were delighted to learn that God was about to deliver them from slavery. But when his talk with Pharaoh backfired and Pharaoh only increased the Israelites' burdens, they blamed Moses for their misery.

"The LORD said to Moses, 'Now you shall see what I will do to Pharaoh. . . .' Therefore say to the children of Israel: 'I am the LORD; I will bring you out from under the burdens of the Egyptians, I will rescue you from their bondage. . . .' So Moses spoke thus to the children of Israel; but they did not heed Moses, because of anguish of spirit and cruel bondage. And the LORD spoke to Moses, saying, 'Go in, tell Pharaoh king of Egypt to let the children of Israel go out of his land.' And Moses spoke before the LORD, saying, 'The children of Israel have not heeded me. How then shall Pharaoh heed me, for I am of uncircumcised lips?' " (Exodus 6:1, 6, 9–12 NKJV).

Uncircumcised lips. Hadn't Moses told God that he was "tongue-tied" and "not very good with words"? Here was the proof. Nobody listened to him. Perhaps a more eloquent speaker would have persuaded Pharaoh. Moses had tried to tell God, but God hadn't listened. On top of it, He was sending him back to Pharaoh for more useless talks.

Of course, God knew that talking was useless, but He wanted to set the stage to demonstrate His incomparable power. Moses, who thought God didn't get it, was the one who truly didn't get it. All he could see was that this approach wasn't working—and he complained. Moses hadn't yet learned two facts: God has "great power" and "his understanding is infinite" (Psalm 147:5 KJV). So he spent his prayer time trying to educate

God on the basic facts.

But eventually, after God had pounded Egypt and Pharaoh into the ground with ten powerful plagues, Pharaoh *did* listen (Exodus 12:31). He just needed some persuasion first. And the Israelites eventually listened (Psalm 78:34). They, too, just needed some persuading.

So often we are like Moses—wondering why God can't understand that His plan just isn't going to work. So we fritter away our prayer time in frustrated efforts to bring Him around to our view. But God doesn't need mortals' explanations. He's not only all-knowing, but all-powerful.

12. A Powerful Prayer of Praise

Prayer is more than just asking God for things, petitioning Him, or interceding for others. Prayer is above all communication with the Lord, and at times we need to communicate our awe and reverence. In the Bible, this often took the form of songs praising God for His mighty acts. "Sing a new song to the LORD, for he has done wonderful deeds. His right hand has won a mighty victory; his holy arm has shown his saving power!" (Psalm 98:1 NLT).

The earliest prayer of praise in the Bible is the song of Moses, composed after God destroyed the Egyptians in the Red Sea:

"Your right hand, LORD, was majestic in power. Your right hand, LORD, shattered the enemy. In the greatness of your majesty you threw down those who opposed you. You unleashed your burning anger; it consumed them like stubble. By the blast of your nostrils the waters piled up. The surging waters stood up like a wall; the deep waters congealed in the heart of the sea. . . . The enemy boasted, 'I will pursue, I will overtake them.' . . . You blew with your breath, and the sea covered them. They sank like lead in the mighty waters. Who among the gods is like you, LORD? Who is like you—majestic in holiness, awesome in glory, working wonders? You stretch out your right hand, and the earth swallows your enemies. In your unfailing love you will lead the people you have redeemed. In your strength you will guide them to your holy dwelling" (Exodus 15:6–8, 9–13 NIV).

Moses' heart was so full of awe and joy at the tremendous miracle God had done that this song spontaneously overflowed. He was singing a prayer to God, and because his words were set to music, the entire nation was able to join in.

In the New Testament, Paul advised believers to speak to themselves "in psalms and hymns and spiritual songs, singing and making melody in [their] heart to the Lord" (Ephesians 5:19 KJV). Not only does God appreciate it when you offer Him sincere praise, but it inspires and strengthens your own spirit. You should thank God when He gains great victories in your life. Thank Him specifically for what He has done. You can even sing your praise to Him.

13. Doubt and Blame

God, visibly present in the pillar of cloud and fire, led the Israelites in their travels (Exodus 13:21–22; 40:36–37). After they miraculously crossed the Red Sea, the cloud guided them south, finally stopping at Rephidim, near Mount Sinai (Horeb), where God would meet them. They had only one problem: there was no water there.

Frustrated, the Israelites began accusing Moses of making a mistake in leading them there. But Moses was only following the cloud. The people then started quarreling with him. Several Israelites demanded, "Is the LORD among us or not?" (Exodus 17:7 NIV). They could see God's cloud. But they wanted more proof: let Him provide water for them. Doubting that He would, they took out their frustrations on Moses, demanding, "Give us water to drink" (Exodus 17:2 NIV).

Moses responded, "Why do you quarrel with me? Why do you put the LORD to the test?" (Exodus 17:2 NIV).

The Israelites then began accusing him. "Why did you bring us up out of Egypt to make us. . .die of thirst?" (Exodus 17:3 NIV). They were mad enough to kill.

Moses went aside and cried to God, "What am I to do with these people? They are almost ready to stone me" (Exodus 17:4 NIV). He had the right idea in getting away to pray, but his prayer was off target. He didn't expect God to prove Himself by providing water. All he wanted was an effective method of crowd control. . .until they could move to someplace that had water.

But God answered, "Take in your hand the staff with which you struck the Nile, and go. I will stand there before you by the rock at Horeb. Strike the rock, and water will come out of it for the people to drink" (Exodus 17:5–6 NIV). So Moses struck the rock and abundant water flowed out.

Moses called the place Meribah [quarreling] because the Israelites quarreled with him. He also called it Massah [testing] because they tested the Lord, demanding He prove His power. The people had their eyes completely off God. But Moses also misjudged the situation, as his prayer revealed.

Sometimes God allows you to be tested severely before He does a miracle. Such tests have a way of revealing what is in your heart.

14. Powerful Intercession

When Moses was on Mount Sinai speaking with God, the Israelites at the base of the mountain made a golden calf and began to worship it with music and lascivious dancing. God was so furious that He said to Moses, "Let Me alone, that My wrath may burn hot against them and I may consume them. And I will make of you a great nation" (Exodus 32:10 NKJV).

But Moses prayed, "LORD, why does Your wrath burn hot against Your people whom You have brought out of the land of Egypt with great power and with a mighty hand? Why should the Egyptians. . .say, 'He brought them out to harm them, to kill them in the mountains, and to consume them from the face of the earth'? Turn from Your fierce wrath, and relent from this harm to Your people" (Exodus 32:11–12 NKJV).

So the Lord relented. But He still intended to punish them, so the next day Moses prayed, "Oh, these people have committed a great sin, and have made for themselves a god of gold! Yet now, if You will forgive their sin—but if not, I pray, blot me out of Your book which You have written" (Exodus 32:31–32 NKJV). If God was going to wipe out the Israelites, Moses didn't want God to make a great nation out of him either.

But God insisted that He would punish only the guilty. He wouldn't wipe out the Israelites in one fell swoop—*now*. However, He promised that He would punish them one day. And He did. The entire older generation died in the desert. Then He sent a plague that day that slew the guiltiest individuals (Exodus 32:35).

Moses knew that the Israelites had sinned seriously and deserved to be punished, so he put his own life on the line when pleading for them. He not only reasoned with God (Exodus

32:11–12), but reminded Him of His promises (v. 13). This was a powerful prayer. Not even Moses could completely shield the Israelites from God's wrath, but his prayer did save the nation from being wiped out.

God still seeks bold, selfless intercessors today. He says, "I sought for a man among them who would. . .stand in the gap before Me on behalf of the land, that I should not destroy it" (Ezekiel 22:30 NKJV). Will you intercede?

15. Longing to See God

Whenever Moses entered the Tent of Meeting (Tabernacle), the pillar of cloud would descend and stand at the entrance of the tent. Then the Lord would speak to Moses face-to-face, just as a man speaks to his friend. One day God told him, "You have found favor in My sight and I have known you by name" (Exodus 33:17 NASB).

God loved him deeply, and Moses loved Him in return. Moses' heart filled with longing to see God in all His splendor, so he implored, "I pray You, show me Your glory!" (Exodus 33:18 NASB).

God replied, "I Myself will make all My goodness pass before you, and will proclaim the name of the LORD before you," but added, "You cannot see My face, for no man can see Me and live!" (Exodus 33:19–20 NASB). God told Moses, "Behold, there is a place by Me, and you shall stand there on the rock; and it will come about, while My glory is passing by, that I will put you in the cleft of the rock and cover you with My hand until I have passed by. Then I will take My hand away and you shall see My back, but My face shall not be seen" (Exodus 33:21–23 NASB).

Many believers since Moses' day have longed to see God. David prayed, "One thing have I desired of the LORD, that will I seek after; that I may dwell in the house of the LORD all the days of my life, to behold the beauty of the LORD" (Psalm 27:4 KJV).

But as Jesus explained, there is a condition: "Blessed are the pure in heart: for they shall see God" (Matthew 5:8 KJV). How can anyone be pure in heart? Believers are washed by the blood of the Lamb. That's why, in heaven, every true Christian will see God. "His servants shall serve him: and they shall see his face" (Revelation 22:3–4 KJV). On earth, even Moses couldn't look directly upon God's face. But one day, all true believers will behold His full glory.

And even now, in direct proportion to how much we seek God, as believers we can drink in increasing levels of God's glory—and it utterly transforms us. "But we all, with open face beholding. . .the glory of the Lord, are changed into the same image from glory to glory" (2 Corinthians 3:18 KJV).

16. Invoking the Priestly Blessing

The Lord told Moses to instruct Aaron and his sons, "This is how you are to bless the Israelites. Say to them: 'The LORD bless you and keep you; the LORD make his face shine on you and be gracious to you; the LORD turn his face toward you and give you peace.' " God added, "So they will put my name on the Israelites, and I will bless them" (Numbers 6:23–27 NIV).

"This is how you are to bless the Israelites." You want to know how to truly bless someone? This is how to do it! Often we repeat this blessing quickly, basking in its transcendent beauty but not meditating on the words or fully comprehending their meaning. So let's have a close look.

When uttering the phrase "The LORD bless you and keep you," you're asking God to act in abundant goodness to someone and supply all their needs, spiritual and physical. You're praying that He will guard them from evil, accidents, and disease.

In praying, "The LORD turn his face toward you" and "the LORD make his face shine on you," you're praying for Him to be intimately involved in their lives, to look with love and favor upon them, to hear and answer their prayers.

Finally, in praying, "The LORD. . .be gracious to you. . .and give you peace," you're asking God to look on them with grace and forgiveness, which brings them peace. You're also praying for them to be focused on God, His love and His power, because Isaiah 26:3 (NKJV) says, "You will keep him in perfect peace, whose mind is stayed on You, because he trusts in You."

And God made a promise concerning this benediction: "So they will put my name on the Israelites, and I *will* bless them" (emphasis added). But be careful: you are *not* to pray such blessings upon evildoers (2 John 1:10–11). To pray, "The

Lord bless you," is to invoke God's name upon someone, and His name only truly marks those who know Him, His children. When speaking of heaven, John wrote, "[His servants] shall see His face, and His name shall be on their foreheads" (Revelation 22:4 NKJV).

In heaven, you'll enjoy the fullness of God's presence and blessing eternally. But God wants you to enjoy a good measure of it now.

17. Prayer for Help

One day everyone in the Israelite camp began weeping: "Oh that someone would give us meat to eat! For we were well-off in Egypt" (Numbers 11:18 NASB). By "someone" they didn't mean God. Instead, they confronted Moses and wailed, "Give us meat that we may eat!" (Numbers 11:13 NASB). They insisted that Moses fulfill their yearning for meat—and now! But of course, he couldn't.

Moses became deeply discouraged. Feeling like a wretched failure, he prayed to God, "Why have You been so hard on Your servant? And why have I not found favor in Your sight, that You have laid the burden of all this people on me? Was it I who conceived all this people? Was it I who brought them forth, that You should say to me, 'Carry them in your bosom as a nurse carries a nursing infant, to the land which You swore to their fathers'? Where am I to get meat to give to all this people? . . . I alone am not able to carry all this people, because it is too burdensome for me. So if You are going to deal thus with me, please kill me at once, if I have found favor in Your sight, and do not let me see my wretchedness" (Numbers 11:11–15 NASB).

God didn't kill Moses. Instead, He said, "Gather for Me seventy men from the elders of Israel. . . . I will take of the Spirit who is upon you, and will put Him upon them; and they shall bear the burden of the people with you, so that you will not bear it all alone" (Numbers 11:16–17 NASB).

This may remind you of your children, or of people at your workplace. Instead of looking to God, they drop their complaints on your desk. But no human can do the impossible. In fact, even taking care of every difficult-but-possible problem is too much for one person. You'll feel like giving up if you shoulder everyone's burdens. You can't "carry them in your bosom." That's why it's important to delegate responsibility to others.

When he felt like a total failure, Moses asked to die. Have you ever felt like that? Thank God He doesn't take us at our word when we pray in deep despair. Instead, He looks beyond our discouragement, sees the problem, and sends a solution.

18. How Can God Do That?

God told the Israelites, "The LORD heard you when you cried, 'Oh, for some meat!'. . . . Now the LORD will give you meat, and you will have to eat it. And it won't be for just a day or two, or for five or ten or even twenty. You will eat it for a whole month until you gag and are sick of it" (Numbers 11:18–20 NLT).

Moses, with his limited understanding, couldn't see how God could provide like that. He said, "There are 600,000 foot soldiers here with me, and yet you say, 'I will give them meat for a whole month!' Even if we butchered all our flocks and herds, would that satisfy them? Even if we caught all the fish in the sea, would that be enough?" (Numbers 11:21–22 NLT). Moses considered the only options he thought available and blurted out his doubt.

The Lord replied, "Has my arm lost its power? Now you will see whether or not my word comes true!" (Numbers 11:23 NLT).

God sent a wind that swept in vast flocks of quail. Every spring they migrate from Africa to Europe and their route crosses the Sinai desert. So God brought *all* the migrating quail at once and began buffeting them with heavy winds. Exhausted birds dropped to the ground inside the camp and for miles in every direction. The Israelites went out and gathered literal tons of quail (Numbers 11:31–32)!

It wasn't a sin that Moses couldn't understand how God would do such a miracle, but he went wrong by limiting God and assuming there were only two ways to end up with as much meat as God said. Either (a) butcher all their flocks and herds, or (b) catch all the fish in the sea. And neither option would last them a month. But all the time, God was planning option c.

The smartest thing Moses could have done was to pray and

ask God what He was going to do. That's what Mary did. When the angel Gabriel told her, "You will conceive in your womb and bring forth a Son," Mary was astonished, so she asked, "How can this be. . . ?" (Luke 1:31, 34 NKJV). So Gabriel explained. Then, satisfied, Mary believed. Moses, too, could have prayed, "How are You going to do this, Lord?"

19. Intercession

The land of Ethiopia (Kush) lay to the south of Egypt, and quite a number of Ethiopians lived in Egypt. As a result, some of them left Egypt with the Israelites. At some point, Moses took an Ethiopian woman for a second wife. This greatly offended Miriam and Aaron, and they led a rebellion against him, saying, "Has the LORD indeed spoken only through Moses? Has He not spoken through us also?" (Numbers 12:2 NKJV). They wanted people to listen to them, not Moses.

But God said to Moses, Aaron, and Miriam, "Come out, you three, to the tabernacle of meeting!" (Numbers 12:4 NKJV). There the Lord came down in the pillar of cloud and rebuked Aaron and Miriam, informing them that Moses was His anointed prophet. It was not for them to judge him. So God asked, "Why then were you not afraid to speak against My servant Moses?" (Numbers 12:8 NKJV).

Then the cloud lifted up from the tabernacle, and before their very eyes, Miriam became leprous, as white as snow. She had obviously been the most outspoken in criticizing Moses, so God made an example of her. Aaron quickly begged forgiveness for his and Miriam's sin and pleaded with Moses to intercede for her.

"So Moses cried out to the LORD, saying, 'Please heal her, O God, I pray!'" (Numbers 12:13 NKJV).

This is one of Moses' shortest prayers, but it was obviously sufficient. We can't read the emotion in his prayer, but we can well imagine it. Despite her criticism of Moses, Miriam was, after all, his older sister, who—as a young girl—had watched over his cradle when he had been set adrift on the crocodile-infested Nile. He had a deep love for her, and it filled his words.

No wonder God listened.

The Lord said that he would heal Miriam. . .but only after she had lived as a leper for seven days. So Miriam was shut out of the camp for one week, and the Israelites didn't continue their journey until she was brought in. Why did God leave her a leper that long? Because she had spearheaded a public rebellion against Moses, and this was a serious sin. God wanted her—and all the Israelites—to understand this clearly. It would take *time* to ponder this deeply.

20. Reminding God of His Mercy

Moses sent twelve spies north into Canaan, and after forty days, they returned. Ten of them reported that there was no way they could defeat the armies of Canaan. This so discouraged the Israelites that they cried, "Would that we had died in this wilderness! Why is the LORD bringing us into this land, to fall by the sword?" (Numbers 14:2–3 NASB). Only Joshua and Caleb insisted that, with God's help, they could conquer the land.

God angrily asked, "How long will they not believe in Me, despite all the signs which I have performed in their midst? I will smite them with pestilence and dispossess them" (Numbers 14:11–12 NASB). He wanted to kill them on the spot.

But Moses prayed, "If You slay this people. . .then the nations who have heard of Your fame will say, 'Because the LORD could not bring this people into the land which He promised them by oath, therefore He slaughtered them in the wilderness.' But now, I pray, let the power of the Lord be great, just as You have declared, 'The LORD is slow to anger and abundant in lovingkindness, forgiving iniquity and transgression. . . .' Pardon, I pray, the iniquity of this people according to the greatness of Your lovingkindness, just as You also have forgiven this people, from Egypt even until now" (Numbers 14:15–19 NASB).

Moses not only told God how bad it would look if He wiped out His people, but he also reminded God that He had, in fact, forgiven the stubborn, doubting Israelites many times already. Why destroy them at this point after having gone though so much with them and bringing them so far?

So the Lord listened to Moses and said, "I have pardoned them. . .*but*. . ." (Numbers 14:20–21 NASB, emphasis added). This was a significant "but." None of the rebels would enter the Promised Land. God wouldn't slay them here and now. He would let them die of old age. But they would all die, and only the younger generation, their children, would march in to conquer Canaan. God declared to the people, "Just as you have spoken in My hearing, so I will surely do to you; your corpses will fall in this wilderness" (Numbers 14:28–29 NASB).

However, the ten fearful spies did die immediately in a plague.

21. Unusual Answer to Prayer

After the older generation had died, it was time for the younger generation to enter Canaan. They requested permission to pass through Edom, but the Edomites refused. So the Israelites were forced to march south though the Arabah, around Edom. There is hardly a more desolate region on earth, and "the soul of the people became very discouraged on the way" (Numbers 21:4 NKJV).

It was stifling hot and bone-dry. There was no water or food. However, God continued to send manna. But the people murmured to Moses, "Why have you brought us up out of Egypt to die in the wilderness? For there is no food and no water, and our soul loathes this worthless bread" (Numbers 21:5 NKJV).

Manna was anything but worthless. It was packed with so much nutritional value that it alone sustained the daily needs of the Israelites. God was so displeased that He sent serpents into their camp, which bit people. Soon they were dying. Realizing their mistake, they hurried to Moses and confessed, "We have sinned, for we have spoken against the LORD and against you; pray to the LORD that He take away the serpents from us" (Numbers 21:7 NKJV). So Moses prayed for them.

The Bible doesn't tell us his words, but we can be sure that Moses asked God to forgive the people, to send the snakes away, and to heal those who'd been bitten. He probably had no idea *how* God would heal. He simply prayed in faith and trusted God to do what only He could do.

Then the Lord instructed him, "Make a fiery serpent, and set it on a pole; and it shall be that everyone who is bitten, when he looks at it, shall live" (Numbers 21:8 NKJV). Moses probably had an Israelite metalworker grab the nearest bronze staff and quickly hammer it into a replica of a serpent. Then they attached it to a tall pole, and everyone who looked at it lived.

God could have healed without it. But in this case, He required a visual symbol. This shows the importance not only of praying, but of listening to God's answer. Prayer involves more than just talking to God. You must also listen to Him—whether He speaks through the Bible or a friend, or impresses a solution on your heart.

22. Don't Pray about This Again

When the children of Israel arrived at the Desert of Zin, they discovered that there wasn't a single drop of water there and began complaining. So God told Moses, "Speak to that rock before their eyes and it will pour out its water" (Numbers 20:8 NIV). God wanted to show His love for the people. But Moses was angry and shouted, "Listen, you rebels, must we bring you water out of this rock?" (Numbers 20:10 NIV). Then Moses struck the rock with his staff—twice—and water gushed out.

The Lord still did the miracle, but Moses had disobeyed. So God informed him, "Because you did not trust in me enough to honor me as holy in the sight of the Israelites, you will not bring this community into the land I give them" (Numbers 20:12 NIV).

Later Moses led the Israelites around Edom to just east of the Jordan River. The Promised Land was so near. But the Lord said to Moses, "Go up this mountain in the Abarim Range and see the land I have given the Israelites. After you have seen it, you too will be gathered to your people" (Numbers 27:12–13 NIV).

But Moses pled, "Sovereign LORD, you have begun to show to your servant your greatness and your strong hand. . . . Let me go over and see the good land beyond the Jordan—that fine hill country and Lebanon" (Deuteronomy 3:24–25 NIV).

The Lord replied, "That is enough. . . . Do not speak to me anymore about this matter. Go up to the top of Pisgah and look west and north and south and east. Look at the land with your own eyes, since you are not going to cross this Jordan" (Deuteronomy 3:26–27 NIV).

When the Israelites doubted, rebelled, and murmured, God repeatedly forgave them. But frequently He still punished them in measure—though not immediately. And this is what He did with Moses. This is the only recorded time when God refused to listen to Moses' prayer and, in fact, ordered him to cease praying about it. God had made His decision, and He didn't want to hear another word on the matter.

Sometimes this will also be the case in your life. Your heart will be set on something, but it won't be God's will for you. So His answer will be no.

23. Praying for a Successor

When you realize that your days are numbered, it sharpens your priorities. It forces you to focus on unfinished business. You try to leave your house in order so that your family won't have to sort through a confused mass of papers to tie up final business and personal matters. And if you're a leader, your thoughts go to who will take your place. This was Moses' concern.

When God told Moses that his time had come to die, he prayed, "O LORD, you are the God who gives breath to all creatures. Please appoint a new man as leader for the community. Give them someone who will guide them wherever they go and will lead them into battle, so the community of the LORD will not be like sheep without a shepherd" (Numbers 27:16–17 NLT).

In answer to his prayer, the Lord told Moses, "Take Joshua son of Nun, who has the Spirit in him, and lay your hands on him. . .and publicly commission him to lead the people. Transfer some of your authority to him so the whole community of Israel will obey him" (Numbers 27:18–20 NLT). So Moses dedicated Joshua as the new leader.

Moses very likely had a good idea that Joshua would be God's choice. After all, Joshua had led the armies of Israel since the Exodus forty years earlier (Exodus 17:8–13). He could definitely "lead them into battle" now. Joshua had been Moses' personal aide from the beginning (Exodus 24:13) and had learned much from him. Plus, wise leadership usually requires an experienced, older man—and Joshua was one of only two old men who God had promised would enter the Promised Land (Numbers 14:29–30).

But rather than assuming that Joshua was the man, Moses

left it open. He had been guilty of assuming things in the past, but now he laid the matter before the Lord and let Him choose. Moses knew that God often did the unexpected, so he was open to God naming someone else. But this time the Lord operated according to Moses' expectations.

God may or may not do exactly what you expect Him to do. So when you pray, don't just present your demand to God and insist that He rubber-stamp it. Give Him space to work.

24. Stop Praying Like That!

After conquering Jericho, the Israelites came to Ai. Since it was a small city, they sent only three thousand men against it. To their shock, the defenders rushed out and killed thirty-six Israelites. Joshua was shaken.

He and the elders lay on the ground before the ark of the covenant all day. Joshua prayed, "Alas, O Lord God, why did You ever bring this people over the Jordan, only to deliver us into the hand of the Amorites, to destroy us? . . . O Lord, what can I say since Israel has turned their back before their enemies? For the Canaanites and all the inhabitants of the land will hear of it, and they will surround us and cut off our name from the earth. And what will You do for Your great name?" (Joshua 7:7–9 NASB).

Then God said, "Get up! Why are you lying on your face like this? Israel has sinned and broken my covenant! They have stolen some of the things that I commanded must be set apart for me. And they have not only stolen them but have lied about it. . . . That is why the Israelites are running from their enemies. . . . I will not remain with you any longer unless you destroy the things among you that were set apart for destruction" (Joshua 7:10–12 NLT).

The Lord then led Joshua to the man who had committed the sin. His name was Achan, and he had taken a bar of gold and some other plunder from Jericho and hidden them under his tent. So Achan and his family were put to death.

When Joshua and the elders were praying, they weren't searching their hearts, asking what sin Israel had committed. The entire day they were asking God why He had done this. Joshua even hinted that the Lord was at fault: "Why did You ever bring this people over the Jordan, *only to* deliver us into the hand of the Amorites?" God's answer, therefore, was abrupt. "Get up!" He commanded. He wanted Joshua to stop praying like that.

It's important to pray during times of trouble, but it's also important to pray *correctly*. It's often wise to say: "Search me, O God, and know my heart: try me, and know my thoughts: and see if there be any wicked way in me" (Psalm 139:23–24 KJV).

25. Short Prayer, Long Answer

God had commanded the Israelites not to make peace treaties with the Canaanites or Amorites, but to fight them and possess their cities and lands. But one day some Amorites from the city of Gibeon arrived at the Israelite camp, claiming to be ambassadors from a distant country. So Joshua made a treaty with them. The Israelites were dismayed three days later when they discovered the deception, but they had to honor their word.

Other Amorites were furious. They decided to annihilate Gibeon for making peace with the enemy. Soon the armies of five kings were besieging them. Gibeon begged Israel to defend them, and after an all-night march, the Israelites struck the Amorites at dawn. The fighting was fierce and lasted all day. It continued to rage even as the sun was setting.

Joshua wanted to finish the battle, so he prayed in front of all the people of Israel, "Sun, stand still over Gibeon; and Moon, in the Valley of Aijalon" (Joshua 10:12 NKJV). So the sun stood still and the moon stayed in place. When God wants to do miracles, He's well able to bend the laws of nature to serve His purposes. Jeremiah exclaimed, "Ah, Lord GOD! Behold, You have made the heavens and the earth by Your great power and outstretched arm. There is nothing too hard for You" (Jeremiah 32:17 NKJV).

The Bible notes: "There has been no day like that, before it or after it, that the LORD heeded the voice of a man; for the LORD fought for Israel" (Joshua 10:14 NKJV). God was intent on defeating the Amorites. As this bizarre day refused to end, the Amorites broke ranks and fled, and God sent a terrific hailstorm—something Joshua hadn't even prayed for—and it pounded the Amorites. In fact, the hail killed more enemies than the Israelites had.

God answered Joshua's prayer so amazingly not only because of his great faith, but because it was God's implicit *will* that the Amorites be defeated. This is an important principle for us to bear in mind. When we pray, "if we ask anything *according to His will*, He hears us. And if we know that He *hears* us, whatever we ask, we know that we *have* the petitions that we have asked of Him" (1 John 5:14–15 NKJV, emphasis added).

26. Polite Prayers of Protest

For seven years in a row, every time it was wheat harvest, the Midianites had swept out of the desert, overrun Israel, and utterly ravaged the land. They had vast flocks and herds that ate all the crops and trampled what they didn't eat. The Israelites were forced to flee their farms for shelters in mountain clefts, caves, and strongholds. In desperation, they cried out to God.

One day the angel of the Lord came and sat under an oak tree in Ophrah where a man named Gideon was secretly threshing wheat to keep it from the Midianites. The angel of the Lord was God Himself in physical form. He had appeared to Abraham centuries earlier, and Abraham had realized that he was the Lord, but Gideon thought that he was simply some man.

God announced, "The LORD is with you, mighty warrior" (Judges 6:12 NIV).

Gideon was doubtful, but at least he was polite about it. "Pardon me, my lord," he replied, "but if the LORD is with us, why has all this happened to us? Where are all his wonders that our ancestors told us about when they said, 'Did not the LORD bring us up out of Egypt?' But now the LORD has abandoned us and given us into the hand of Midian" (Judges 6:13 NIV).

The Lord said, "Go in the strength you have and save Israel out of Midian's hand. Am I not sending you?" (Judges 6:14 NIV).

Strength? Gideon wondered. "Pardon me, my lord," he replied, "but how can I save Israel? My clan is the weakest in Manasseh, and I am the least in my family" (Judges 6:15 NIV).

"The LORD answered, 'I will be with you, and you will strike down all the Midianites' " (Judges 6:16 NIV). Sure enough, when Gideon finally got up the courage to lead an army against them, "Midian was subdued before the Israelites and did not raise its head again. During Gideon's lifetime, the land had peace forty years" (Judges 8:28 NIV).

Gideon can certainly be excused for not recognizing God. The Lord also overlooked his self-doubt. Gideon didn't feel up to the task, and his conversation with God was honest and humble. That's very likely why God chose him, to show what He could do with a limited, weak mortal. Remember, even Moses didn't feel up to the task God had for him.

27. Laying Out Fleeces

Gideon eventually suspected that the "man" speaking with him was God, so he said, "Show me a sign that it is You who speak with me" (Judges 6:17 NASB).

Then Gideon prepared a goat and bread. God said, "Take the meat and the unleavened bread and lay them on this rock" (Judges 6:20 NASB). He did. Then God touched them with His staff, and fire blazed from the rock and consumed them. Then He vanished. Gideon exclaimed, "Alas, O Lord GOD! For now I have seen the angel of the LORD face to face." The Lord said, "Peace to you. . .you shall not die" (Judges 6:22–23 NASB).

Later, as Gideon was preparing for battle, he said, "If You will deliver Israel through me, as You have spoken, behold, I will put a fleece of wool on the threshing floor. If there is dew on the fleece only, and it is dry on all the ground, then I will know that You will deliver Israel through me, as You have spoken" (Judges 6:36–37 NASB). Sure enough, when he arose early the next morning and squeezed the fleece, he drained a bowl full of water from it.

Then Gideon said, "Do not let Your anger burn against me . . .please let me make a test once more with the fleece, let it now be dry only on the fleece, and let there be dew on all the ground" (Judges 6:39 NASB). Again, God did a miracle. It was dry only on the fleece, and dew was on all the ground.

After God had vaporized Gideon's sacrifice and bread, then vanished, Gideon *knew* that He was God Almighty. Some criticize Gideon for asking for additional proof that God would be with him. After all, God had already plainly said He would be.

While it's true that Gideon was fearful and hesitant, remember that God never rebuked him for it. He knew his weakness and worked with him. In fact, God later gave him another sign to encourage him, one Gideon hadn't even asked for (Judges 7:9–15).

It's scriptural to "lay fleeces before the Lord," to request signs to help determine what His will is. Just remember that you must keep your word and accept the sign you asked for. Don't casually flip a coin then only accept the "answer" if it's the one you were hoping for.

28. Samson's Prayers

Samson is known for his astonishing feats of strength, not for his prayers. Nevertheless, this amazing strongman prayed in times of need. After slaughtering one thousand Philistine soldiers with a donkey's jawbone, Samson became so thirsty that he was at the point of death. He prayed to the Lord, "You have given this great deliverance by the hand of Your servant; and now shall I die of thirst and fall into the hand of the uncircumcised?" So God split a hollow place, water came out, and Samson drank and revived (Judges 15:18–19 NKJV).

Samson prayed his most famous prayer after Delilah betrayed him to the Philistines. They cut off his hair, and his great strength left him; then they blinded him. Sometime after, the Philistines gathered to offer a sacrifice to Dagon their god, boasting that he had delivered Samson into their hands. So they brought Samson from prison and made him perform for them. This probably consisted of them repeatedly knocking the poor blind man down.

Then they stationed him between the pillars that supported the temple roof. All the lords of the Philistines were up on the roof—about three thousand men and women. The temple below was also full of people. Then Samson called to the Lord, saying, "O Lord GOD, remember me, I pray! Strengthen me, I pray, just this once, O God, that I may with one blow take vengeance on the Philistines for my two eyes!" (Judges 16:28 NKJV).

Samson placed his hands on the two pillars, one on his right and the other on his left. He finished his prayer saying, "Let me die with the Philistines!" (Judges 16:30 NKJV). He then pushed with all his might, and the entire temple collapsed. The Philistines that Samson killed at his death were more than all those he had killed in his life. And with their leaders dead, the Philistines began to lose their control over Israel.

Samson knew that his astonishing strength came from God, so he ultimately depended on Him, not his muscles. You, too, must seek God's face and pray and patiently wait for Him to act. "He gives power to the weak, and to those who have no might He increases strength. Even the youths shall faint and be weary, and the young men shall utterly fall, but those who wait on the LORD shall renew their strength" (Isaiah 40:29–31 NKJV).

29. Praying When Deeply Discouraged

A terrible crime had been committed in Gibeah, a city in the tribe of Benjamin: a man's concubine had been abused all night and died in the morning. The armies of Israel were summoned to decide what to do about this. They sent a delegation to Benjamin, demanding that they hand over the criminals, but the Benjamites refused. Instead, they prepared for war.

So the Israelites prayed to God, " 'Who of us is to go up first to fight against the Benjamites?' The LORD replied, 'Judah shall go first' " (Judges 20:18 NIV). The ensuing battle was a disaster. The Benjamites wiped out 22,000 men of Israel.

Stunned, the Israelites wept before God until evening and inquired of the Lord. Weren't the Benjamites in the wrong? Weren't the armies of Israel doing right in trying to avenge an injustice? Why then had God allowed such a defeat? So they prayed, " 'Shall we go up again to fight against the Benjamites, our fellow Israelites?' The LORD answered, 'Go up against them' " (Judges 20:23 NIV). The Israelites encouraged each other and went out to battle again. But to their shock, they were *again* defeated. The Benjamites killed 18,000 more men.

This time the whole army sat weeping before the Lord. They were deeply discouraged, so they fasted until evening and presented offerings to the Lord. Then the Israelites prayed, " 'Shall we go up again to fight against the Benjamites, our fellow Israelites, or not?' The LORD responded, 'Go, for tomorrow I will give them into your hands' " (Judges 20:28 NIV).

The Israelites went out to battle again. This time they set an ambush against Gibeah, and after the Benjamites rushed out to fight, the Israelites attacked and burned their unguarded city. Then they attacked the Benjamites, who were routed and fled.

It took tremendous faith to rise up and fight the Benjamites the third time. Many people would have given up by then, thinking that God had abandoned them. When things go wrong and God doesn't seem to be answering your prayers, the temptation to stop trying can be great. You may question whether you heard from God in the first place. But if God's answer remains constant, don't give up! You just need to keep praying, keep trying, and keep believing God.

30. Praying in Anguish

There was a man named Elkanah who had two wives. His wife Peninnah had several children, but Hannah had none, and Peninnah taunted her over this, reducing her to tears. Once when they were visiting the tabernacle, Hannah, filled with sorrow, got up to pray. "Hannah was in deep anguish, crying bitterly as she prayed to the Lord. And she made this vow: 'O Lord of Heaven's Armies, if you will look upon my sorrow and answer my prayer and give me a son, then I will give him back to you. He will be yours for his entire lifetime' " (1 Samuel 1:10–11 NLT).

Eli the priest saw her praying, but though her lips were moving, no sound was coming out of her mouth. He thought she was drunk and rebuked her, but when she explained that she was praying out of deep anguish of soul, Eli said, "Go in peace! May the God of Israel grant the request you have asked of him" (1 Samuel 1:17 NLT).

God heard Hannah's prayer and gave her a son, and she named him Samuel. She kept her word, and when Samuel was still a small child, she brought him to the tabernacle to serve the Lord. Every time she visited him, Eli would bless her and Elkanah, saying, "May the Lord give you other children to take the place of this one she gave to the Lord" (1 Samuel 2:20 NLT). God answered this prayer, too, and Hannah conceived and gave birth to three more sons and two daughters.

Hannah's silent prayer of anguish is reminiscent of what Paul wrote: "The Spirit also helps in our weaknesses. For we do not know what we should pray for as we ought, but the Spirit Himself makes intercession for us with groanings which cannot be uttered" (Romans 8:26 NKJV). Often "groanings which cannot be uttered" are requests that cannot be refused. But like Hannah, you may need to persevere in prayer about these things, year after year.

There will be times when the burdens and sorrows you bear will seem intolerable. Perhaps you constantly pour out your heart with tears for an errant child or agonize over a broken relationship. It may seem that your oft-repeated requests are falling on deaf ears, but God hears, and in due time He will answer.

31. Hannah Praises God

When Samuel was about four years old, Hannah and Elkanah brought him to Eli, and she said, "I am the woman who stood here beside you, praying to the LORD. For this boy I prayed, and the LORD has given me my petition which I asked of Him. So. . .as long as he lives he is dedicated to the LORD" (1 Samuel 1:26–28 NASB).

Then Hannah was anointed by the Spirit to proclaim a beautiful prophecy:

"My heart exults in the LORD; my horn [strength] is exalted in the LORD, my mouth speaks boldly against my enemies, because I rejoice in Your salvation. There is no one holy like the LORD, indeed, there is no one besides You, nor is there any rock like our God. . . . Even the barren gives birth to seven, but she who has many children languishes. . . . The LORD makes poor and rich; He brings low, He also exalts. He raises the poor from the dust, He lifts the needy from the ash heap to make them sit with nobles, and inherit a seat of honor. . . . He keeps the feet of His godly ones, but the wicked ones are silenced in darkness; for not by might shall a man prevail" (1 Samuel 2:1–2, 5, 7–9 NASB).

Then Hannah and Elkanah went home, and Samuel stayed and ministered to the Lord.

There is a striking similarity between Hannah's prophetic prayer of praise and the Magnificat given by Mary many centuries later (see Luke 1:46–55). In both cases, deeply spiritual women were promised a child. Both sons were dedicated to God's service. Samuel grew up to be Israel's greatest judge; Jesus was the long-awaited Messiah. And both boys were "growing in stature and in favor both with the LORD and with men" (1 Samuel 2:26 NASB; see Luke 2:52).

This story clearly demonstrates that God responds to the prayers of the humble—those who are of little account in man's eyes—and mightily uses them for His glory. Hannah wasn't an educated woman, but she was deeply spiritual, and her testings had drawn her close to God. If you seem to be nobody special, be encouraged: God sees you, He loves you, and your prayers can move His hand to do great miracles.

32. Praying for God to Speak

Samuel faithfully served the Lord. Now, there were almost
no prophets in those days, and God rarely spoke. And it so
happened one night, before the lamp of God went out in the
tabernacle where the ark of the covenant was, that Eli was lying
down in his chamber and the boy Samuel was lying in his room.
Then the Lord called Samuel's name. He answered, "Here I am!"
(1 Samuel 3:4 NKJV). There was no answer, so he got up and ran
to Eli.

Entering his chamber, Samuel said, "Here I am, for you
called me." But Eli answered, "I did not call; lie down again"
(1 Samuel 3:5 NKJV). Puzzled, Samuel walked back to his room
and returned to bed.

Then the Lord called again, "Samuel!" Again Samuel arose,
went to Eli, and said, "Here I am, for you called me." Eli answered,
"I did not call, my son; lie down again" (1 Samuel 3:6 NKJV).

Then the Lord called Samuel the third time. Again he arose,
went to Eli, and said, "Here I am, for you did call me." Then Eli
realized that God had called the boy. So Eli said to him, "Go, lie
down; and it shall be, if He calls you, that you must say, 'Speak,
Lord, for Your servant hears' " (1 Samuel 3:8–9 NKJV). Samuel
went back and lay down.

Then the Lord came and stood in Samuel's room and called
again, "Samuel! Samuel!" And Samuel answered, "Speak, for
Your servant hears" (1 Samuel 3:10 NKJV).

The Lord told Samuel that He would judge the aged priest
Eli and his sons for their sins. God had sent a prophet in the
past to warn Eli, but he hadn't repented or obeyed (1 Samuel
2:27–36). God judged Eli and his sons some years later then
used Samuel to lead the people back to Him.

God still speaks today—not usually audibly, like He did to Samuel, but in "a still small voice" (1 Kings 19:12 KJV), impressing a message on your heart. Also, Jesus promised, "[The Holy Spirit] will teach you everything and will remind you of everything I have told you" (John 14:26 NLT). So God frequently brings a passage from the Bible to your mind.

But you have to yield your will to God. One of the best things you can do is sincerely pray, "Please speak, Lord. I'm listening and will obey You."

33. Prayer in the Cave of Adullam

The title to Psalm 142 reads: "A maskil of David. When he was in the cave. A prayer (NIV)." This makes it one of David's earliest psalms, written when he was hiding in the Cave of Adullam (1 Samuel 22:1), near the city of Adullam. This short psalm is an intense, emotional prayer. David wrote:

"I cry aloud to the LORD; I lift up my voice to the LORD for mercy. I pour out before him my complaint; before him I tell my trouble. When my spirit grows faint within me, it is you who watch over my way. In the path where I walk people have hidden a snare for me. Look and see, there is no one at my right hand; no one is concerned for me. I have no refuge; no one cares for my life. I cry to you, LORD; I say, 'You are my refuge, my portion in the land of the living.' Listen to my cry, for I am in desperate need; rescue me from those who pursue me, for they are too strong for me. Set me free from my prison, that I may praise your name" (Psalm 142:1–7 NIV).

David probably moved to the cave when the rainy season began, when life out in the open was miserable. For the next few months, he and his men hunkered down in the damp cavern. In Israel, it often rains heavily for three days nonstop. You might think that living in a cave is fun, but David complained that it was like a prison (v. 7). Yes, David complained, but he poured out his complaint to God, not people (v. 2).

David had been a much-loved, highly praised hero in Israel. Now he was vilified, and King Saul and his army were hunting him, seeking to kill him. He'd been forced to flee, leaving his wife Michal behind. It was in this context that he prayed to God, "You are my refuge, my portion in the land of the living." God was about all David had left. So he looked to Him for help.

David was deeply discouraged, yet he prayed, "When my spirit grows faint within me, it is you who watch over my way." He knew that God was with him. You, too, can be assured of this fact: "I will never abandon you" (Hebrews 13:5 NLT).

34. David Seeks Precise Guidance

One day David and his men and all their wives and children packed up all their belongings and left the Cave of Adullam. They traveled south and camped out in the Forest of Hereth. After they had been there a short while, they heard disturbing news: an army of Philistines was attacking the Israelite city of Keilah, a few miles to the south.

"David asked the LORD, 'Should I go and attack them?' 'Yes, go and save Keilah,' the LORD told him. But David's men said, 'We're afraid even here in Judah. We certainly don't want to go to Keilah to fight the whole Philistine army!' So David asked the LORD again, and again the LORD replied, 'Go down to Keilah, for I will help you conquer the Philistines' " (1 Samuel 23:2–4 NLT).

So David and his men marched to Keilah, defeated the Philistines, and rescued the people there. However, Saul soon learned where David was, so he mobilized his entire army to go to Keilah.

But David learned of Saul's plan and prayed, "O LORD, God of Israel, I have heard that Saul is planning to come and destroy Keilah because I am here. Will the leaders of Keilah betray me to him? And will Saul actually come as I have heard? O LORD, God of Israel, please tell me." David was desperate to know, so God told him, "He will come." David asked again, "Will the leaders of Keilah betray me and my men to Saul?" The Lord answered, "Yes, they will betray you" (1 Samuel 23:10–12 NLT).

With such clear answers, David knew he had to leave immediately. So he and his men left the city and began roaming the countryside. Word reached Saul that David had escaped, so he didn't go to Keilah after all.

You probably wish *you* could hear such clear, specific answers. It would make life a whole lot easier and prevent losses and disasters if you could simply hear from God what to do. The good news is, God has promised to guide you, too. You just have to pray wholeheartedly then wait patiently for His answer. "Trust in the LORD with all your heart, and lean not on your own understanding; in all your ways acknowledge Him, and He shall direct your paths" (Proverbs 3:5–6 NKJV).

35. Prayer in the Jaws of Death

David and his men lurked in the barren hill country in the Wilderness of Ziph at Horesh. Saul sought him day after day, but David was aware that Saul was hunting him, so he kept one step ahead of him.

"Then the Ziphites came to Saul at Gibeah, saying, 'Is David not hiding with us in the strongholds at Horesh. . . ? Now then, O king, come. . .and our part shall be to surrender him into the king's hand' " (1 Samuel 23:19–20 NASB). Saul was delighted and told them to find out all David's hiding places and bring him word. Then he'd come.

It was at this point that David, desperate for help, wrote Psalm 54. The title reads, "A Maskil of David, when the Ziphites came and said to Saul, 'Is not David hiding himself among us?' " David prayed:

"Save me, O God, by Your name, and vindicate me by Your power. Hear my prayer, O God; give ear to the words of my mouth. For strangers have risen against me and violent men have sought my life; they have not set God before them. Selah. Behold, God is my helper; the Lord is the sustainer of my soul. He will recompense the evil to my foes; destroy them in Your faithfulness. . . . I will give thanks to Your name, O LORD, for it is good. For He has delivered me from all trouble, and my eye has looked with satisfaction upon my enemies" (Psalm 54:1–7 NASB).

When Saul and his men came, some Israelites told David, and he went to the Wilderness of Maon. Saul heard where he had gone, pursued him, and was soon breathing down his neck. Saul and his army were racing along one side of the mountain, and David and his men were scrambling around the other side. David was hurrying to escape because Saul and his army were surrounding him and his men to seize them.

But just when Saul had nearly caught them, a messenger rushed up to Saul, out of breath, saying, "Hurry and come, for the Philistines have made a raid on the land" (1 Samuel 23:27 NASB). Saul had no choice. He abandoned pursuing David and hurried north to battle the Philistines.

At the last possible minute, God answered David's prayer and rescued him.

36. Prayer for Protection and Guidance

When Saul was pursuing David and many Israelites were ready to betray him, David wasn't sure where to turn or whom to trust. He complained, "There is but a step between me and death" (1 Samuel 20:3 NKJV). So he prayed:

"Hear my prayer, O LORD, give ear to my supplications! . . . For the enemy has persecuted my soul. . . . Therefore my spirit is overwhelmed within me; my heart within me is distressed . . . . Answer me speedily, O LORD; my spirit fails! Do not hide Your face from me, lest I be like those who go down into the pit. Cause me to hear Your lovingkindness in the morning, for in You do I trust; cause me to know the way in which I should walk, for I lift up my soul to You. Deliver me, O LORD, from my enemies; in You I take shelter. Teach me to do Your will, for You are my God; Your Spirit is good. Lead me in the land of uprightness" (Psalm 143:1, 3, 4, 7–10 NKJV).

You may not have an enemy hunting you, but you may be wandering in the wilderness of a troubled economy, not knowing which way to turn or what decision to make. One way leads to success and another way leads to great hardship. . .but both choices look identical. So like David, you pray desperately.

"Teach me to do Your will, for You are my God." Even more vital than making good financial decisions, you need to know how to live by godly principles. If the Lord is your God, the center of your life, you will seek His will. And He will show you.

"Cause me to know the way in which I should walk, for I lift up my soul to You." After making certain that your spiritual life is on the right foundation, you can confidently ask God to lead you in practical matters. And He has promised: "Commit your way to the LORD, trust also in Him, and He shall bring it to pass" (Psalm 37:5 NKJV).

"Deliver me, O LORD, from my enemies; in You I take shelter." The Bible promises, "Because you have made the LORD . . .your dwelling place, no evil shall befall you" (Psalm 91:9–10 NKJV). But you must continually *abide* in God for this promise to be fulfilled.

37. Being Encouraged to Pray

David and his men had left their wives and children in Ziklag, and in their absence, Amalekite raiders attacked, burned the town, and took everything. When David's men returned, they were stunned. They wept loudly until they had no more power to weep. They were so grieved that they spoke of stoning him. David was greatly distressed, but instead of giving up and going under, he "strengthened himself in the LORD his God" (1 Samuel 30:6 NKJV).

David then asked God, "Shall I pursue this troop? Shall I overtake them?" The Lord answered, "Pursue, for you shall surely overtake them and without fail recover all" (1 Samuel 30:8 NKJV).

So David and his men began tracking the raiders. Along the way, they found a half-dead Egyptian, and after questioning him, David learned that he had been an Amalekite slave, but his master had abandoned him when he became sick. The Egyptian confessed that they had raided Ziklag.

David asked him, "Can you take me down to this troop?" The Egyptian answered, "Swear to me by God that you will neither kill me nor deliver me into the hands of my master, and I will take you down to this troop" (1 Samuel 30:15 NKJV). So he led them to the Amalekite camp, and there they were, spread out and off guard, eating and drinking and dancing, rejoicing over all the spoil they had taken.

David's men attacked them from twilight until the evening of the next day. They utterly routed the Amalekites and recovered all that they had carried away. Nothing was lacking that had been taken from them. They recovered everything. What a powerful answer to prayer!

Sometimes you'll suffer a disaster and feel overwhelmed.

Perhaps you sinned and failed God, and now the devil is trying to convince you that God is obliged to shut out your prayer and punish you—so you should just call it quits and not bother praying. This is one of his cleverest lies. Instead, do like David did: "David strengthened himself in the LORD," reminding himself that God loved him—and not only that, but that God could do the impossible. Once he was assured of those two facts, David was encouraged to pray and believe for a miracle.

So refuse to give up, refuse to stop trusting the Lord, and turn to Him in prayer.

38. David's Song of Praise

After he defeated the Amalekites, and with Saul dead, David went to Hebron where he was crowned king of Judah. Then he became embroiled in a seven-year civil war with the northern tribes. No sooner was David proclaimed king of all Israel than the Philistines invaded. David defeated them but then was forced to battle several other nations. Despite many troubles and some near defeats, David gained great victories.

"David sang this song to the LORD on the day the LORD rescued him from all his enemies and from Saul. He sang: 'The LORD is my rock, my fortress, and my savior; my God is my rock, in whom I find protection. He is my shield, the power that saves me, and my place of safety. He is my refuge, my savior, the one who saves me from violence. I called on the LORD, who is worthy of praise, and he saved me from my enemies' " (2 Samuel 22:1–4 NLT).

David prayed, "O LORD, you are my lamp. The LORD lights up my darkness. In your strength I can crush an army. . . . You have given me your shield of victory; your help has made me great. You have made a wide path for my feet to keep them from slipping. . . . You have armed me with strength for the battle; you have subdued my enemies under my feet. . . . For this, O LORD, I will praise you among the nations; I will sing praises to your name. You give great victories to your king; you show unfailing love to your anointed" (2 Samuel 22:29–30, 36–37, 40, 50–51 NLT).

David was indeed marvelously helped, and he knew that God deserved the praise for his great victories. But you may wonder if this triumphant psalm possibly applies to your life. You may feel defeated, frustrated, and desperate for a breakthrough. But remember, David, too, was frequently on the verge of defeat (2 Samuel 22:5–7, 18–19). But he prayed, and God repeatedly brought success.

Paul wrote, "Now thanks be to God who *always* leads us in triumph in Christ" (2 Corinthians 2:14 NKJV, emphasis added). And " 'For Your sake we are killed all day. . . .' Yet *in all these things* we are more than conquerors through Him who loved us" (Romans 8:36–37 NKJV, emphasis added).

39. God, Fulfill Your Promises

One day David told the prophet Nathan that he desired to build a temple for the Lord. The next day, Nathan returned to David with a message from God: one of his sons—not David himself—would build God a house. But God would build *David's* house. Nathan prophesied, " 'The LORD also declares to you that the LORD will make a house for you. . . . Your house and your kingdom shall endure before Me forever; your throne shall be established forever' " (2 Samuel 7:11, 16 NASB).

Deeply moved, David prayed, "O LORD God, the word that You have spoken concerning Your servant and his house, confirm it forever, and do as You have spoken. . .and may the house of Your servant David be established before You. . . . For You, O LORD of hosts, the God of Israel, have made a revelation to Your servant, saying, 'I will build you a house'; therefore Your servant has found courage to pray this prayer to You. Now, O Lord GOD, You are God, and Your words are truth, and You have promised this good thing to Your servant. Now therefore, may it please You to bless the house of Your servant, that it may continue forever before You. For You, O Lord GOD, have spoken; and with Your blessing may the house of Your servant be blessed forever" (2 Samuel 7:25–26, 27–29 NASB).

Sure enough, God saw to it that David's house (his throne and kingdom) endured eternally in Jesus the Messiah (Psalm 89:3–4; Luke 1:32).

Notice that David repeated his request four times. Some people think David's entire prayer was unnecessary—that he needn't have bothered asking God even once. Since God had already promised that David's house would endure forever, why request Him to make good on this promise? But the Bible says,

"We are labourers together with God" (1 Corinthians 3:9 KJV). God wants us to stir ourselves up in prayer and implore Him to fulfill His promises.

After all, God had told Saul, "You have not kept the commandment of the LORD your God. . . . For now the LORD would have established your kingdom over Israel forever. But now your kingdom shall not continue" (1 Samuel 13:13–14 NKJV). David knew that he, too, could lose the promise through disobedience, negligence, and lack of prayer, and he didn't want to take a chance on that.

40. Repenting of Serious Sins

One spring evening, when his army was away at war, David was walking on the flat roof of his palace. He happened to look down into a nearby courtyard and saw a naked beauty named Bathsheba. David had his servants bring her, and he committed adultery with her. When she became pregnant, he tried to get her husband, Uriah, to sleep with her so he'd think the child was his. When that failed, David had Uriah killed (2 Samuel 11:1–27).

The prophet Nathan confronted David about these crimes, and overcome with remorse, he repented and prayed:

"Have mercy upon me, O God, according to Your loving-kindness; according to the multitude of Your tender mercies, blot out my transgressions. Wash me thoroughly from my iniquity, and cleanse me from my sin. For I acknowledge my transgressions, and my sin is always before me. . . . Behold, I was brought forth in iniquity, and in sin my mother conceived me. . . . Wash me, and I shall be whiter than snow. . . . Hide Your face from my sins, and blot out all my iniquities. Create in me a clean heart, O God, and renew a steadfast spirit within me. Do not cast me away from Your presence, and do not take Your Holy Spirit from me. Restore to me the joy of Your salvation, and uphold me by Your generous Spirit. . . . The sacrifices of God are a broken spirit, a broken and a contrite heart—these, O God, You will not despise" (Psalm 51:1–3, 5, 7, 9–12, 17 NKJV).

The Law said that adulterers should be stoned and murderers were to be executed, but God heard David's heartfelt prayer and had mercy on him. Nevertheless, because he'd had Uriah killed with the sword, Nathan informed David, "The sword shall never depart from your house. . . . The LORD also has put away your sin; you shall not die. However. . .the child also who is born to you shall surely die" (2 Samuel 12:10, 13–14 NKJV). All these things happened.

God can and does forgive sin—even very serious sins. He promised, "Though your sins are like scarlet, they shall be as white as snow; though they are red like crimson, they shall be as wool" (Isaiah 1:18 NKJV). But you must sincerely repent and ask for forgiveness.

41. Praying about Frenemies

David's son Absalom wanted to be king, so he organized a conspiracy and won many Israelites to his side. He marched on Jerusalem, but David was warned, fled the city, and marshaled his troops across the Jordan River. Absalom assembled his army and followed, and the two armies clashed in the Forest of Ephraim. Despite David's order not to harm Absalom, Joab executed him. The battle was over. God had once again protected David (2 Samuel 15:10–13; 17:24–26; 18:1–17).

David wrote a short psalm just before the battle, proclaiming that he trusted God to protect him and wouldn't fear. The title to Psalm 3 reads, "A psalm of David. When he fled from his son Absalom" NIV. In this psalm, David prayed:

"LORD, how many are my foes! How many rise up against me! Many are saying of me, 'God will not deliver him.' But you, LORD, are a shield around me, my glory, the One who lifts my head high. I call out to the LORD, and he answers me from his holy mountain. I lie down and sleep; I wake again, because the LORD sustains me. I will not fear though tens of thousands assail me on every side. Arise, LORD! Deliver me, my God! Strike all my enemies on the jaw; break the teeth of the wicked. From the LORD comes deliverance. May your blessing be on your people" (Psalm 3:1–8 NIV).

David had instructed Joab, "Be gentle with the young man Absalom for my sake" (2 Samuel 18:5 NIV). However, he had prayed to God, "Strike all my enemies on the jaw; break the teeth of the wicked" (Psalm 3:7 NIV). Likely David only wished God to strike the men of Israel following Absalom, but he had prayed, "Strike *all* my enemies." So Absalom died.

The most outstanding lesson from David's prayer, however,

is his tremendous trust in the Lord. Knowing that God was a shield around him and wouldn't allow him to be harmed even though multitudes surrounded and assailed him, David confidently held his head up and refused to give in to despair. He also lay down and slept peacefully, without tossing and turning and worrying all night.

David probably prayed nonstop every day, but this psalm is a clear snapshot that captures his heart and shows what all his other prayers were like.

42. Praying to a Merciful God

David conquered the entire land of Canaan—something even Joshua hadn't done—and expanded Israel's borders from Egypt in the south to the Euphrates River in the north. He had taken it with a limited number of men because God strengthened him mightily. But in his latter years he seems to have become concerned about holding this great empire together.

So David ordered a census to find exactly how many men he had and exactly how strong his army was. But after he had numbered his soldiers, David's conscience began to bother him. He prayed, "I have sinned greatly by taking this census. Please forgive my guilt, LORD, for doing this foolish thing" (2 Samuel 24:10 NLT).

The prophet Gad told him, "This is what the LORD says: I will give you three choices. . . . Will you choose three years of famine throughout your land, three months of fleeing from your enemies, or three days of severe plague throughout your land?" (2 Samuel 24:12–13 NLT).

"I'm in a desperate situation!" David replied. "But let us fall into the hands of the LORD, for his mercy is great. Do not let me fall into human hands" (2 Samuel 24:14 NLT).

So God sent a plague on Israel. It lasted for three days, and 70,000 people died. But as the angel was preparing to destroy Jerusalem, David saw him, and prayed, "I am the one who has sinned and done wrong! But these people are as innocent as sheep—what have they done? Let your anger fall against me and my family" (2 Samuel 24:17 NLT). So the Lord relented and ordered the angel to stop.

The angel stopped on the hill belonging to Araunah the Jebusite. Gad then instructed David to build an altar on that spot, so he built an altar and sacrificed burnt offerings and peace offerings. Then the Lord stopped the plague.

David had declared of God, "His mercy is great," and knowing this essential truth gave him the courage to pray for mercy, even though his sin had been serious. Centuries later, Jonah echoed this thought: "I know that You are a gracious and merciful God, slow to anger and abundant in lovingkindness, One who relents from doing harm" (Jonah 4:2 NKJV). It's vital that you, too, are convinced of God's mercy and goodwill, as it will have a direct bearing on how you pray.

43. Lord, Don't Be Silent

As David grew older, he became more serious about life and prayed:

> *My heart was hot within me, while I was musing the fire burned; then I spoke with my tongue: "LORD, make me to know my end and what is the extent of my days; let me know how transient I am. Behold, You have made my days as handbreadths, and my lifetime as nothing in Your sight; surely every man at his best is a mere breath. . . . And now, Lord, for what do I wait? My hope is in You. Deliver me from all my transgressions; make me not the reproach of the foolish. I have become mute, I do not open my mouth, because it is You who have done it. Remove Your plague from me; because of the opposition of Your hand I am perishing. With reproofs You chasten a man for iniquity. . .surely every man is a mere breath. . . . Hear my prayer, O LORD, and give ear to my cry; do not be silent at my tears; for I am a stranger with You, a sojourner like all my fathers. Turn Your gaze away from me, that I may smile again before I depart and am no more."*
>
> PSALM 39:3–5, 7–13 NASB

Sickness has a way of making you appreciate health like nothing else. You realize how frail you are, after all. The endless youth and good health and strength you once took for granted, and assumed would last forever, have come to an end. You realize how short life is and want to make every day count.

At times like this, you pour out your heart to God, saying, "Hear my prayer, O LORD, and give ear to my cry; do not be silent at my tears." Anyone who has prayed repeatedly for a desperate need knows how trying it can be to face deafening silence when there is no apparent answer. It leaves you wondering if God has heard, if He even cares. He does care, He is moved by your tears, and He will answer in His time and in the way He deems best.

David prayed, "My heart was hot within me. . .then I spoke with my tongue." It's God's Spirit who stirs up your heart and moves you to pray.

44. Prayer When Sick and Weak

At some point during his reign, David was quite sick. Most likely this occurred during his last decade. David's enemies were delighted that he was afflicted and wished he would die. Many Israelites had joined Absalom's rebellion, and although they had been defeated and David was still king, powerful men were now his enemies.

David wrote: "All who hate me whisper together against me; against me they devise my hurt. 'An evil disease,' they say, 'clings to him. And now that he lies down, he will rise up no more' " (Psalm 41:7–8 NKJV). But David said to God, "You will not deliver him to the will of his enemies. The LORD will strengthen him on his bed of illness; You will sustain him on his sickbed" (Psalm 41:2–3 NKJV).

It was around this time that David prayed: "Have mercy on me, O LORD, for I am weak; O LORD, heal me, for my bones are troubled. My soul also is greatly troubled; but You, O LORD— how long? Return, O LORD, deliver me! Oh, save me for Your mercies' sake! For in death there is no remembrance of You; in the grave who will give You thanks? I am weary with my groaning. . .I drench my couch with my tears. My eye wastes away because of grief; it grows old because of all my enemies" (Psalm 6:2–7 NKJV).

David then confidently declared: "Depart from me, all you workers of iniquity; for the LORD has heard the voice of my weeping. The LORD has heard my supplication; the LORD will receive my prayer. Let all my enemies be ashamed and greatly troubled" (Psalm 6:8–10 NKJV).

David was weary, troubled, and grieving. He bluntly asked the Lord how long before He healed him. As with so many of

David's psalms, this was a very honest prayer.

After David cried out desperately for God to heal him he said, "The LORD will receive my prayer." He was old and weak and sick but trusted God to heal him and raise him up, saying, "The LORD will strengthen him on his bed of illness." And God did. David remained Israel's ruler until he died a natural death at seventy years of age. At that time he was no longer sick—simply too old to keep up his body heat (1 Kings 1:1).

45. Solomon Prays for Wisdom

Shortly after Solomon became king, he went to Gibeon to sacrifice to God. That night the Lord appeared to him in a dream and said, "Ask what you wish Me to give you" (1 Kings 3:5 NASB).

This was one of the only times in the Bible when God offered to give someone whatever they asked for. Many Christians have the mistaken impression that God is at their beck and call, like a genie, ready to grant their every wish. They think they can command Him. But we must understand that He is Almighty God, to be worshiped and obeyed. He does not obey human whims.

Solomon could have requested things for his personal benefit, but he said, "O LORD my God, You have made Your servant king in place of my father David, yet I am but a little child; I do not know how to go out or come in. Your servant is in the midst of Your people which You have chosen, a great people who are too many to be numbered or counted. So give Your servant an understanding heart to judge Your people to discern between good and evil. For who is able to judge this great people of Yours?" (1 Kings 3:7–9 NASB).

God was so pleased that Solomon had asked for wisdom in order to better serve the needs of God's people that He said, "I have done according to your words. Behold, I have given you a wise and discerning heart, so that there has been no one like you before you, nor shall one like you arise after you. I have also given you what you have not asked, both riches and honor, so that there will not be any among the kings like you all your days" (1 Kings 3:12–13 NASB).

God is still delighted to give His children wisdom. The

Bible promises, "If any of you lacks wisdom, let him ask of God, who gives to all generously and without reproach, and it will be given to him" (James 1:5 NASB). God also delights to give other gifts as well, which is why Paul wrote that believers are to "earnestly desire the best gifts" (1 Corinthians 12:31 NKJV).

"A spiritual gift is given to each of us so we can help each other" (1 Corinthians 12:7 NLT). And this was the very reason that Solomon asked for wisdom.

46. Solomon's Prayer of Dedication

For seven years, Solomon directed the building of God's temple, and when it was completed, he dedicated it to God and prayed:

> *Give attention to your servant's prayer and his plea for mercy, LORD my God. . . . May your eyes be open toward this temple night and day, this place of which you said, "My Name shall be there," so that you will hear the prayer your servant prays toward this place. Hear the supplication of your servant and of your people Israel when they pray toward this place. Hear from heaven, your dwelling place, and when you hear, forgive. . . . When your people Israel have been defeated by an enemy because they have sinned against you, and when they turn back to you. . .praying and making supplication to you in this temple, then hear from heaven and forgive the sin of your people Israel. . . . When the heavens are shut up and there is no rain because your people have sinned against you, and when they pray toward this place. . .then hear from heaven and forgive the sin of your servants, your people Israel. Teach them the right way to live, and send rain on the land. . . . When famine or plague comes to the land, or blight or mildew, locusts or grasshoppers, or when an enemy besieges them in any of their cities, whatever disaster or disease may come, and when a prayer or plea is made by anyone among your people Israel. . .then hear from heaven, your dwelling place. Forgive and act.*
>
> 1 KINGS 8:28–30, 33–39 NIV

When Solomon finished praying, fire swept down from heaven and consumed the burnt offering and the sacrifices, and the glory of the Lord filled the temple. The priests couldn't enter the sanctuary because the Lord's glory completely filled it (2 Chronicles 7:1–2). Then the Lord said to Solomon, "I have heard the prayer and plea you have made before me; I have consecrated this temple, which you have built, by putting my Name there forever. My eyes and my heart will always be there" (1 Kings 9:3 NIV).

Solomon prayed a comprehensive prayer of dedication, asking the Lord to hear the people's prayers, mercifully forgive their sins, and restore them. God responded that His presence would abide in the temple for those very purposes.

47. The Prayer of Jabez

There was a man in the land of Judah named Jabez who was more honorable than any of his brothers. But his mother had named him Jabez (He Will Cause Pain) because his birth had been so painful. Jabez is famous for praying to God, "Oh, that you would bless me and enlarge my territory! Let your hand be with me, and keep me from harm so that I will be free from pain" (1 Chronicles 4:10 NIV).

The good news is, God granted his request! Jabez requested several things in this short prayer, so let's look at them one by one.

"That you would bless me!" It's perfectly acceptable to pray for God to bless you. It's not necessarily selfish. After all, Jesus taught His disciples to pray that God would supply their daily bread (Matthew 6:11), and Paul prayed that God would "supply all your needs from his glorious riches" (Philippians 4:19 NLT). You are to continually bless others, so it stands to reason that you are to bless *yourself* as well.

"That you would. . .enlarge my territory!" Originally, this would have meant to acquire more fields and land, to be materially prosperous. These days, Jabez might have been asking for God to enlarge his business prospects *or* his ministry. After all, Christians often understand the phrase, "Enlarge the place of your tent, stretch your tent curtains wide" (Isaiah 54:2 NIV), to apply to spiritual endeavors as well as to financial ventures.

"Let your hand be with me." With this request, Jabez was asking God to work with him in all he did. The Bible tells us, "The LORD was with Joseph, giving him success in everything he did" (Genesis 39:3 NLT). We desperately need God. Moses prayed to Him, "If Your Presence does not go with us, do not bring us up from here" (Exodus 33:15 NKJV).

"Keep me from harm so that I will be free from pain." According to the NIV, Jabez simply wanted to avoid accidents and pain. However, the NKJV translates the phrase as, "Keep me from evil, that I may not cause pain!" That makes more sense. His mother had named him "He Will Cause Pain," so he prayed that he would be kept from doing evil, so he *wouldn't* cause pain to others. These are all good requests.

48. Praying in Peace and War

When Asa became king, he loved the Lord and walked closely with Him. He removed the altars of pagan gods, destroyed the high places, and broke down the idols. Maachah, the queen mother, had made an obscene image of Asherah, so Asa deposed her and burned this image to ashes. He also commanded all Judah to seek God and obey Him (2 Chronicles 14:2–15; 1 Kings 15:13).

At this time, "great turmoil was on all the inhabitants of the lands" and "nation was destroyed by nation" (2 Chronicles 15:5–6 NKJV), but for ten years Judah was quiet. Asa knew that this peace was a result of worshiping God. He said, "We have sought the LORD our God. . .and He has given us rest on every side" (2 Chronicles 14:7 NKJV).

But Asa knew that trouble might come eventually, so he wisely used this time to fortify Judah's cities and build up an army of 580,000 men. Then one day the Cushites (from south of Egypt) invaded with an army of 1 million men (2 Chronicles 14:9 NKJV). Asa marshaled his army and met them in a valley to the west of Hebron.

Asa was badly outnumbered, so he cried out, "LORD, it is nothing for You to help, whether with many or with those who have no power; help us, O LORD our God, for we rest on You, and in Your name we go against this multitude. O LORD, You are our God; do not let man prevail against You!" (2 Chronicles 14:11 NKJV).

The Lord mightily answered Asa's prayer and struck the Cushites. Panic-stricken, they fled, and Asa's army pursued them as far as Philistia. The Cushites were "broken before the LORD and His army" (2 Chronicles 14:13 NKJV).

God answered Asa's many prayers down through the years, miraculously giving him tranquility when all other lands were suffering turmoil and war. And when the world's troubles eventually did spill over into Judah, Asa continued praying, and God continued answering. The Lord answered Asa's desperate prayer because Asa was in the habit of faithfully praying. He didn't operate in his own strength and turn to God only when trouble came. His devotion to prayer allowed Asa to pray such powerful prayers in emergencies—and get answers.

49. Public Prayer in Desperate Times

During the reign of Jehoshaphat, three nations—Ammon, Moab, and Edom—invaded Judah. He was fearful and proclaimed a fast, so people came from all over Judah to seek the Lord.

Jehoshaphat stood in the temple court and prayed: "O LORD, the God of our fathers, are You not God in the heavens? And are You not ruler over all the kingdoms of the nations? Power and might are in Your hand so that no one can stand against You. Did You not, O our God, drive out the inhabitants of this land before Your people Israel and. . .they have lived in it, and have built You a sanctuary there for Your name, saying, 'Should evil come upon us, the sword, or judgment, or pestilence, or famine, we will stand before this house and before You (for Your name is in this house) and cry to You in our distress, and You will hear and deliver us.' Now behold, the sons of Ammon and Moab and Mount Seir, whom You did not let Israel invade when they came out of the land of Egypt. . .see how they are rewarding us. . . . O our God, will You not judge them? For we are powerless before this great multitude who are coming against us; nor do we know what to do, but our eyes are on You" (2 Chronicles 20:6–12 NASB).

It was a desperate hour, one that required godly, courageous leadership—and Jehoshaphat rose to the occasion, publicly declaring his trust in God.

Then a Levite named Jahaziel prophesied, "Thus says the LORD to you, 'Do not fear or be dismayed because of this great multitude, for the battle is not yours but God's. . . . You need not fight in this battle. . . . Tomorrow go out to face them, for the LORD is with you" (2 Chronicles 20:15, 17 NASB).

Early the next morning they went out to face the invaders,

and Jehoshaphat sent singers out ahead of the army. When they began singing and praising, the Lord turned Ammon, Moab, and Edom against one another, and they killed one another. When the army of Judah arrived at the spot, there were corpses all over the ground. When you believe God is going to bring victory, you do well to praise Him ahead of time.

50. Perplexed, Accusing Prayers

Once during a prolonged drought, the Lord told Elijah to go to the village of Zarephath in Phoenicia, and as he arrived, he saw a woman gathering sticks. He asked her to bring him some water and bread, but she replied that she had only a handful of flour and a tiny bit of cooking oil left. But when Elijah promised that God would provide for her if she shared it with him, she believed. And her flour and olive oil didn't run out for many months.

But then her son became sick. He grew worse and finally died. The grieving widow wailed, "O man of God, what have you done to me? Have you come here to point out my sins and kill my son?" (1 Kings 17:18 NLT).

Elijah took the body, carried it to his room, and laid it on his bed. Perplexed and desperate, he cried out, "O LORD my God, why have you brought tragedy to this widow who has opened her home to me, causing her son to die?" Then he prayed, "O LORD my God, please let this child's life return to him" (1 Kings 17:20–21 NLT).

"The LORD heard Elijah's prayer" (1 Kings 17:22), and the child revived. Then Elijah returned him to his astonished and grateful mother.

Elijah had focused on the widow's recent righteous deeds. But she had focused on her past guilt. She assumed she was being judged for former sins. This very likely wasn't a factor. The *main* reasons God allowed the boy to die were to show His tender love for a foreign widow, to demonstrate His great power, and to inspire their faith.

Also, the widow viewed her son's death as final. Elijah didn't accept that. He believed that his all-powerful God could raise the dead.

Note that Elijah asked God, "Why have you brought tragedy. . .causing her son to die?" There was a tinge of accusation in his prayer. He wondered if God had acted unjustly. Still, he knew that God was good and twice called Him, "O LORD *my* God."

God often hears accusatory prayers today, even from His children. He knows that such prayers come from lives overflowing with grief. He's aware that mortals often can't understand what He's doing, so He listens past the ignorance and anger to the heart of our prayers.

51. When God Has Determined to Act

In Elijah's day, many Israelites worshiped both God *and* Baal, so Elijah asked, "How long will you waver between two opinions? If the LORD is God, follow him; but if Baal is God, follow him" (1 Kings 18:21 NIV). Then Elijah gave a challenge: both he and Baal's priests would sacrifice a bull and place the meat on the wood of their altars—but not set fire to it. Then the priests would call on Baal, while Elijah called on the Lord. Whoever answered by fire was the true God.

The priests prepared a bull and prayed to Baal for several hours but received no response. At noon Elijah began to taunt, "Shout louder! . . . Perhaps he is deep in thought, or busy, or traveling. Maybe he is sleeping and must be awakened" (1 Kings 18:27 NIV). They continued praying frantically until evening, but no answer came.

Then Elijah prepared the Lord's altar, cut a bull in pieces, and laid it on the wood. He had the people dump twelve large jars of water on the offering and wood. Then Elijah prayed: "LORD, the God of Abraham, Isaac and Israel, let it be known today that you are God in Israel and that I am your servant and have done all these things at your command. Answer me, LORD, answer me, so these people will know that you, LORD, are God" (1 Kings 18:36–37 NIV).

Immediately, fire blazed down, devouring the sacrifice, the wood, the stones, the dust, and the water. All the people shouted, "The LORD—he is God! The LORD—he is God!" (1 Kings 18:39 NIV).

This test wasn't Elijah's idea. He did all this "at God's command," because God had already determined to do the miracle. So Elijah didn't need to petition Him a long time. He simply needed to step onstage and introduce the Lord—and no sooner had he done that than God unleashed His power.

You probably wish that God always answered requests as suddenly and dramatically. But often you need to persevere in prayer. It can be puzzling when God answers some prayers swiftly yet seems not to answer other prayers despite your repeated, anguished petitions. You may wonder if those requests simply aren't His will. They very likely *may* be God's will, but it just isn't the time to answer them.

52. Fervent, Repeated Prayers

Years earlier, before the contest on Mount Carmel, "Elijah. . . prayed earnestly that it would not rain; and it did not rain on the land for three years and six months" (James 5:17 NKJV). He had told King Ahab, "As the LORD God of Israel lives. . . there shall not be dew nor rain these years, except at my word" (1 Kings 17:1 NKJV). Sure enough, the drought had continued unbroken all this time. But after God sent down fire, Elijah knew it was time for the dearth to end.

Elijah told Ahab, "There is the sound of abundance of rain," so while Ahab went to eat, Elijah climbed to the top of Carmel. There he bowed down and prayed. Then he said to his servant, "Go up now, look toward the sea." He went up, but came back with the message: "There is nothing." Seven times Elijah said, "Go again" (1 Kings 18:41–43 NKJV).

But when his servant came back the seventh time, he reported, "There is a cloud, as small as a man's hand, rising out of the sea!" Elijah ordered, "Say to Ahab, 'Prepare your chariot, and go down before the rain stops you.' " As he was speaking, the sky became black with clouds and there was wind and heavy rain (1 Kings 18:44–45 NKJV).

Elijah had prayed for a drought, and it didn't rain for years. "He prayed again, and the heaven gave rain" (James 5:18 NKJV). While it's true that Elijah had tremendous faith, the same power of God is available to believers today. After all, "Elijah was a man with a nature like ours" (James 5:17 NKJV). The key is to pray fervently. "The effective, fervent prayer of a righteous man avails much" (James 5:16 NKJV).

Often we—like Elijah—need to bring a petition before the Lord numerous times. God sent down fire after Elijah had prayed the briefest of prayers *once*, but it took multiple requests to bring on rain, even though that, too, was God's express will. Remember, even *before* praying, Elijah had heard "the sound of abundance of rain."

You can't put God in a box and create a formula for how He *will* or *must* answer prayer. God may answer after just one prayer or after many prayers. He may require only a short prayer or have you persist in your request for years.

53. Praying Defeatist Prayers

If Elijah had hoped that his victory on Mount Carmel would cause a nationwide revival, he was mistaken. When Jezebel threatened to kill him, the people melted away instead of rallying to protect him. Alone, in mortal danger, Elijah's courage failed also, and he ran. He fled Israel, crossed Judah, and disappeared into the vast desert south of Beersheba, apparently taking no food along.

As he trekked through that desolate region, his energy was drained by the heat and by waves of depression. Exhausted, he slumped under a juniper tree and prayed, "It is enough; now, O Lord, take my life, for I am not better than my fathers" (1 Kings 19:4 NASB). Despairing, he fell asleep.

Then an angel touched him and said, "Arise, eat" (1 Kings 19:5 NASB). Elijah awoke and discovered a loaf of bread baked on hot stones and a jar of water. So he ate and drank and lay down again. The angel awoke him a second time, saying, "Arise, eat, because the journey is too great for you" (1 Kings 19:7 NASB). So he ate and drank again, and in the strength of that miraculous food, he walked forty days to the mountain of God.

Not only did God not take Elijah's life then as he'd requested, but God saw to it that he *never* died—one of only two men taken to heaven alive (2 Kings 2:11). And God's immediate response to his defeatist prayer was to get some high-energy food into him to get his blood sugar up and help lift him from his negative mood.

Some Christians think that if they pray something negative, then they've irreversibly cursed themselves, and both God and the devil will be sure to destroy them. Now, certainly it's best not to pray defeatist prayers. But like a wise, caring parent, God says no to such requests. In fact, He doesn't answer many prayers Christians pray, even for good things that aren't best for them.

Have you ever felt like giving up—on a job, on a marriage, on a strong-willed child—yet afterward repented and asked God for the strength to keep going? You, too, are headed for the mountain of God, and "the journey is too great for you." So cry out to God. Let Him breathe life into you. Let Him strengthen you. He will help you make it.

54. Hearing from God

Elijah arrived at Mount Horeb in the Sinai Desert. It was there that God had come with thunder, lightning, fire, and an earthquake (Exodus 19:16–18) when He met with Moses and the Israelites centuries earlier. Elijah, too, wanted his "Moses moment."

Instead, God asked, "What are you doing here, Elijah?" (1 Kings 19:9 NIV).

Elijah complained, "I have been very zealous for the Lord God Almighty. The Israelites have rejected your covenant, torn down your altars, and put your prophets to death with the sword. I am the only one left, and now they are trying to kill me too" (1 Kings 19:10 NIV).

God ordered, "Go out and stand on the mountain. . .for the Lord is about to pass by" (1 Kings 19:11 NIV).

Then a powerful wind shattered the rocks, but the Lord was not in the wind. An earthquake battered the mountain, but the Lord was not in the earthquake. Then a fire swept the mountain, but the Lord was not in the fire. And after the fire came a gentle whisper—what the King James Version calls "a still small voice (1 Kings 19:12)."

Again God asked, "What are you doing here, Elijah?" (1 Kings 19:13 NIV).

Elijah then gave God the exact same answer. Apparently, during his long, long hike to Horeb, he had gone over and over again what he wanted to tell God. So he repeated his carefully rehearsed speech verbatim.

But God replied, "Go back the way you came" (1 Kings 19:15 NIV). In other words, "You didn't need to come all the way here to speak to me." God wasn't being insensitive to His discouraged prophet. He knew Elijah would be fine. He just needed an attitude adjustment. Elijah had wanted God to speak loud and clear in a dramatic earthquake with thunder and fire and judgment. But God chose to reveal Himself in a gentle whisper.

God told Elijah what to do next, for the time was coming to judge his enemies. As for his complaint that he was the only faithful Israelite left, the Lord informed Elijah that seven thousand others had also not bowed to Baal. From these, he was to choose Elisha to help him in his ministry.

You, too, may often be frustrated by God's silences and His mysterious dealings. You long for a "Moses moment" when He reveals Himself dramatically. But God usually guides you through life with still, small, faint, almost imperceptible directions.

55. Open My Eyes, Lord

When the king of Aram was at war with Israel, he would say to his officers, "We will mobilize our forces at such and such a place." But Elisha the prophet of God repeatedly warned the king of Israel, "Do not go near that place" (2 Kings 6:8–9 NLT).

The king of Aram became furious. He demanded of his officers, "Which of you is the traitor? Who has been informing the king of Israel of my plans?" An officer replied, "It's not us. . . Elisha, the prophet in Israel, tells the king of Israel even the words you speak in the privacy of your bedroom!" The king then ordered, "Go and find out where he is." And the report came back: "Elisha is at Dothan" (2 Kings 6:11–13 NLT). So the king of Aram sent a great army with many chariots and horses to surround the city by night.

When Elisha and his servant got up the next morning, his servant looked off the city wall, and there were troops, horses, and chariots everywhere. "What will we do now?" he cried. "Don't be afraid!" Elisha answered. "For there are more on our side than on theirs!" When his servant gave a blank look, Elisha prayed, "O Lord, open his eyes and let him see!" (2 Kings 6:15–17 NLT). Then God opened his eyes and he saw that the hillside around Elisha was filled with horses and chariots of fire.

Then Elisha prayed, "O Lord, please make them blind" (2 Kings 6:18 NLT). So the Lord struck the Arameans with blindness. They couldn't *see* Elisha, let alone arrest him, so eventually they went back to Aram without him.

Elisha lived in the supernatural realm, in close contact with God. That's why he was able to pray such short, direct prayers and receive immediate answers. Now Elisha had an unusually powerful anointing and was a mighty miracle worker, and though the same power of God is available to work on your behalf, He may not do miracles of the same great magnitude for you.

But you *can* still emulate Elijah: he loved God and spent a great deal of time praying to Him. So God revealed things to him and answered his prayers. God promises, "Because he has set his love upon Me. . .he shall call upon Me, and I will answer him" (Psalm 91:14–15 NKJV).

56. When God Doesn't Hear Prayer

Sailors often have good reason to pray. "Those who go down to the sea in ships. . .see the works of the LORD. . . . He commands and raises the stormy wind, which lifts up the waves of the sea. . . . Then they cry out to the LORD in their trouble, and He brings them out of their distresses. He calms the storm" (Psalm 107:23–25, 28–29 NKJV).

In Jonah's day, some sailors found themselves in exactly this situation. God had told Jonah to go to Nineveh and warn them of impending judgment, but Jonah didn't want to take a chance that God might spare Nineveh, so he fled the opposite direction—to Tarshish at the western end of the known world.

The ship began sailing across the Mediterranean, but not far out, the Lord sent a great wind, so that the ship was nearly broken up in the tempest. The sailors cried out to their individual gods. They woke Jonah and said, "Arise, call on your God; perhaps your God will consider us, so that we may not perish" (Jonah 1:6 NKJV).

But Jonah had a problem. God wasn't listening to his prayers because he had stubbornly disobeyed Him.

When Jonah confessed to the sailors what he'd done, they asked, "What shall we do to you that the sea may be calm for us?" Jonah said, "Pick me up and throw me into the sea; then the sea will become calm" (Jonah 1:11–12 NKJV). They did, and the sea ceased raging. Then the men feared the Lord, offered a sacrifice to Him, and vowed to Him. God heard their prayers, but He wasn't listening to Jonah—not until Jonah repented.

Sin often prevents God from answering prayer. It was true in Jonah's day, and it's true today. "Surely the arm of the LORD is not too short to save, nor his ear too dull to hear. But. . .your sins have hidden his face from you, so that he will not hear" (Isaiah 59:1–2 NIV).

If you're constantly praying but not receiving an answer, it's wise to check your heart to see if you're somehow sinning against God. He could simply be testing your patience and resolve. Or the devil might be fighting you. But the problem might be sin.

57. Nothing to Do but Pray

When Jonah told the sailors to toss him into the raging sea, he was certain he would die. He may even have been okay with that. At least he wouldn't have to go to Nineveh and warn them. But God wasn't done yet. Suddenly a gigantic fish surfaced, and Jonah disappeared straight into the sea monster's gaping maw.

Seconds later, he was in its belly, in utter darkness, covered with slime. . .and trapped. Mere moments before, he had admitted, "I know that on account of me this great storm has come upon you" (Jonah 1:12 NASB). Now he had plenty of time to pray about that. He could do nothing but pray. But apparently for some time Jonah didn't repent. Finally, he cried out to God:

"I called out of my distress to the LORD, and He answered me. I cried for help from the depth of Sheol; You heard my voice. For You had cast me into the deep, into the heart of the seas, and the current engulfed me. All Your breakers and billows passed over me. So I said, 'I have been expelled from Your sight. Nevertheless I will look again toward Your holy temple'. . . . I descended to the roots of the mountains. . .but You have brought up my life from the pit, O LORD my God. While I was fainting away, I remembered the LORD, and my prayer came to You. . . . I will sacrifice to You with the voice of thanksgiving. That which I have vowed I will pay. Salvation is from the LORD" (Jonah 2:2–4, 6–7, 9 NASB).

The instant Jonah repented, the Lord commanded the fish and it surfaced on a beach, probably on the coast near Ugarit, and vomited Jonah up. Chastened, Jonah headed inland to Nineveh and, when he eventually arrived there, warned them of their imminent doom.

God often gives His children a time-out when they disobey

Him. "There were those who dwelt in darkness. . .prisoners in misery and chains, because they had rebelled against the words of God. . . . They stumbled and there was none to help. Then they cried out to the Lord in their trouble; He saved them out of their distresses" (Psalm 107:10–13 NASB).

58. A Royal Prayer

When Hezekiah was ruler of Judah, Sennacherib the Assyrian king sent his officers with a huge army to Jerusalem. The Assyrian field commander called to Hezekiah's officials on the wall, "Do not listen to Hezekiah, for he is misleading you when he says, 'The LORD will deliver us.' Has the god of any nation ever delivered his land from the hand of the king of Assyria?" (2 Kings 18:32–33 NIV).

Later the commander sent Hezekiah a letter: "Do not let the god you depend on deceive you when he says, 'Jerusalem will not be given into the hands of the king of Assyria.' Surely you have heard what the kings of Assyria have done to all the countries, destroying them completely. And will you be delivered? Did the gods of the nations that were destroyed by my predecessors deliver them?" (2 Kings 19:10–12 NIV).

King Hezekiah read the letter. Deeply offended and grieved, he went to the temple and spread it out before the Lord. Then he prayed a truly royal prayer:

"LORD, the God of Israel, enthroned between the cherubim, you alone are God over all the kingdoms of the earth. You have made heaven and earth. Give ear, LORD, and hear; open your eyes, LORD, and see; listen to the words Sennacherib has sent to ridicule the living God. It is true, LORD, that the Assyrian kings have laid waste these nations and their lands. They have thrown their gods into the fire and destroyed them, for they were not gods but only wood and stone, fashioned by human hands. Now, LORD our God, deliver us from his hand, so that all the kingdoms of the earth may know that you alone, LORD, are God" (2 Kings 19:15–19 NIV).

Hezekiah's beautiful prayer extolled God for His immense

power and reminded Him that the Assyrians had insulted Him—and God answered dramatically. That night the angel of the Lord cut down 185,000 men in the Assyrian camp. When Hezekiah and his people awoke the next morning, they saw endless corpses. The surviving Assyrians broke camp and returned to Nineveh.

Hezekiah didn't doubt that God would act, though he probably had no idea what He would do. He prayed in faith, fully expecting God to defend His name and reputation from mockery. And He did.

59. Hezekiah Prays to Live

Some time after the miraculous defeat of the Assyrians, King Hezekiah became deathly ill from a boil. Certain he might die, Hezekiah said this prayer:

"In the prime of my life, must I now enter the place of the dead? Am I to be robbed of the rest of my years? . . . Never again will I see the LORD GOD while still in the land of the living. Never again will I see my friends or be with those who live in this world. . . . I waited patiently all night, but I was torn apart as though by lions. Suddenly, my life was over. Delirious, I chattered like a swallow or a crane. . . . My eyes grew tired of looking to heaven for help. I am in trouble, Lord. Help me!" (Isaiah 38:10–11, 13–14 NLT).

But it looked like God was *not* going to help him. The prophet Isaiah brought him this message: "This is what the LORD says: Set your affairs in order, for you are going to die" (2 Kings 20:1 NLT).

"When Hezekiah heard this, he turned his face to the wall and prayed to the LORD, 'Remember, O LORD, how I have always been faithful to you and have served you single-mindedly, always doing what pleases you.' "That's all he managed to say before he "broke down and wept bitterly" (2 Kings 20:2–3 NLT). A short while earlier he had dictated an eloquent prayer. Now he was so overcome with emotion that he could barely speak.

But God heard. Isaiah had already left the middle courtyard, but God stopped him and sent him back with this message: "This is what the LORD. . .says: I have heard your prayer and seen your tears. I will heal you, and three days from now you will get out of bed and go to the Temple of the Lord. I will add fifteen years to your life, and I will rescue you and this city from the king of Assyria" (2 Kings 20:5–6 NLT).

"Then Isaiah said, 'Make an ointment from figs.' So Hezekiah's servants spread the ointment over the boil, and Hezekiah recovered!" (2 Kings 20:7 NLT).

God appreciates it when you pour out your heart to Him in eloquent prayer. Hezekiah's prayer against the Assyrians was anointed, and God answered powerfully. But there will be times when you will be so distraught that you can barely speak. And God answers *those* prayers also.

60. Prayer in Messiah's Kingdom

Isaiah prophesied that one day the Messiah would reign over all the earth (Isaiah 11:1–10), and in that day God's people would pray:

"O LORD, I will praise You; though You were angry with me, Your anger is turned away, and You comfort me. Behold, God is my salvation, I will trust and not be afraid; 'For YAH, the LORD, is my strength and song; He also has become my salvation.' Therefore with joy you will draw water from the wells of salvation. And in that day you will say: 'Praise the LORD, call upon His name; declare His deeds among the peoples, make mention that His name is exalted. Sing to the LORD, for He has done excellent things; this is known in all the earth. Cry out and shout, O inhabitant of Zion, for great is the Holy One of Israel in your midst!' " (Isaiah 12:1–6 NKJV).

These events will only be fully realized in the Millennium, but if you love Jesus the Messiah, His reign has already begun in your heart, and you can pray this now.

It's wonderful to have peace with God. The wrath of God abides on those who don't know Him (John 3:36). God *was* angry with you, but now, because of your faith in Jesus' atoning death, His anger is turned away.

Now you can pray: "God is my salvation, I will trust and not be afraid." Jesus came to "release those who through fear of death were all their lifetime subject to bondage" (Hebrews 2:15 NKJV). Anxiety and fear also disappear from your life. "There is no fear in love; but perfect love casts out fear" (1 John 4:18 NKJV).

In the place of worry you can have joy: "With joy you will draw water from the wells of salvation." Jesus promised, "The water I give them will become in them a spring of water welling up to eternal life" (John 4:14 NIV).

Knowing that Jesus has saved you gives you happiness. "Sing to the LORD. . . . Cry out and shout." You can be happy even during trying circumstances, for you "are kept by the power of God through faith for salvation. . . . In this you greatly rejoice, though now for a little while. . .you have been grieved by various trials" (1 Peter 1:5–6 NKJV).

61. Questioning God

The prophet Habakkuk was grieved by the violent, selfish lifestyle of the Jewish people and the way the rich oppressed the poor. So he prayed:

"How long, O Lord, will I call for help, and You will not hear? I cry out to You, 'Violence!' yet You do not save. Why do You make me see iniquity, and cause me to look on wickedness? Yes, destruction and violence are before me. . . . The law is ignored and justice is never upheld. For the wicked surround the righteous; therefore justice comes out perverted" (Habakkuk 1:1–4 NASB).

God answered, "Behold, I am raising up the Chaldeans, that fierce and impetuous people who march throughout the earth" (Habakkuk 1:6 NASB). The Chaldeans (Babylonians) had already conquered many eastern nations, and God warned that they'd soon invade Judah to punish her for her sins.

But this presented a new dilemma for Habakkuk. The Babylonians were pagans—they were wicked, ruthless, and treacherous. So he prayed, "You, O Lord, have appointed them to judge; and You, O Rock, have established them to correct." Then Habakkuk pointed out the conundrum: "Your eyes are too pure to approve evil, and You can not look on wickedness with favor. Why do You look with favor on those who deal treacherously?" (Habakkuk 1:12–13 NASB).

God answered that after He had used the Babylonians to judge Judah and other nations, it would be *their* turn to be judged: "Because you have looted many nations, all the remainder of the peoples will loot you—because of human bloodshed and violence done to the land" (Habakkuk 2:8 NASB).

When the Babylonian armies finally came, they ruled

Judah with restraint at first, and Jeremiah admonished the Jews to submit to their rule. But after the Jews repeatedly rebelled against them, the Babylonians swept into Judah, besieged Jerusalem, and inflicted severe retribution on the Jews.

Life is often messy, and situations sometimes seem so complex that we can't understand how *any* solution God proposes will fix things. It seems as if His answer will only bring new problems. But God is all-wise and able to sort out even the knottiest problems and bring a just solution in the end. So He's okay with our questions. Just be aware that we may not fully understand what He's doing, even if He explains. So trust Him!

62. A Lament

Judah had rebelled against God, worshiping Baal and other gods. They had refused to repent and return to God, even though Jeremiah had warned them for decades that disaster was coming. Sure enough, judgment day arrived: the Babylonians attacked and Jerusalem was surrounded. Inside the walls, the Jews suffered terrible famine and plague; outside, they were mercilessly slaughtered.

Finally, Jerusalem fell to the besiegers, and enemies like the Edomites rejoiced at its destruction. Jeremiah, who had survived the disaster locked in a dank prison, staggered out into the sunlight to behold scenes of utter desolation. He lamented, claiming the punishment of his people as his own:

"See, LORD, how distressed I am! I am in torment within, and in my heart I am disturbed, for I have been most rebellious. Outside, the sword bereaves; inside, there is only death. People have heard my groaning, but there is no one to comfort me. All my enemies have heard of my distress; they rejoice at what you have done. . . . Let all their wickedness come before you; deal with them as you have dealt with me because of all my sins. My groans are many and my heart is faint" (Lamentations 1:20–22 NIV).

God's people had abandoned Him, so God abandoned them. Jeremiah cried out, "You, LORD, reign forever; your throne endures from generation to generation. Why do you always forget us?" (Lamentations 5:19–20 NIV).

But in the midst of his lament, Jeremiah held out hope: "I called on your name, LORD, from the depths of the pit. You heard my plea: 'Do not close your ears to my cry for relief.' You came near when I called you, and you said, 'Do not fear' " (Lamentations 3:55–57 NIV). Jeremiah added, "Because of the

Lord's great love we are not consumed, for his compassions never fail" (Lamentations 3:22).

God will also be with *you* in your darkest hour when you're condemned, afflicted, and feel utterly forsaken. You can call out to God from the mess you've made of your life, and He will hear you. No matter how far you've strayed from Him, no matter how deeply you've sinned—even if He's punishing you right now—He never completely removes His love and mercy. He will never utterly forsake you, and He promises, "For a small moment have I forsaken thee; but with great mercies will I gather thee" (Isaiah 54:7 KJV).

63. National Confession and Repentance

At key points in history, godly men have stood up to intercede for their nations, confessing the sins of their people as their own. Daniel was one such man. The time had come for God to restore His people to their land, so Daniel prayed:

> *O Lord, great and awesome God, who keeps His covenant and mercy with those who love Him, and with those who keep His commandments, we have sinned and committed iniquity, we have done wickedly and rebelled, even by departing from Your precepts and Your judgments. Neither have we heeded Your servants the prophets. . . . O Lord, to us belongs shame of face, to our kings, our princes, and our fathers, because we have sinned against You. To the Lord our God belong mercy and forgiveness, though we have rebelled against Him. We have not obeyed the voice of the LORD. . .therefore the curse and the oath written in the Law of Moses the servant of God have been poured out on us. . . . O Lord, according to all Your righteousness, I pray, let Your anger and Your fury be turned away from Your city Jerusalem. . . . God, hear the prayer of Your servant, and his supplications, and for the Lord's sake cause Your face to shine on Your sanctuary, which is desolate. O my God. . .we do not present our supplications before You because of our righteous deeds, but because of Your great mercies. O Lord, hear! O Lord, forgive! O Lord, listen and act!*
>
> DANIEL 9:4–6, 8–11, 16–19 NKJV

Daniel's lengthy prayer was probably composed on paper. It is a masterpiece of intercession, squarely admitting his people's sins and God's righteousness in judging them, while reminding God of His mercy and forgiveness. Note the powerful line: "We do not present our supplications before You because of our righteous deeds, but because of Your great mercies." Daniel was throwing himself completely upon God's mercy.

God answered him, describing not only his people's restoration, but the coming of the Messiah: "From the going forth of the command to restore and build Jerusalem until Messiah the Prince, there shall be seven weeks and sixty-two weeks; the street shall be built again, and the wall" (Daniel 9:25 NKJV).

Daniel's prayer provided the needed breakthrough, and from that day on, God worked to restore His people.

64. Ezra Confesses His People's Sins

When the leading priest Ezra arrived in Judah, he learned that many people—even priests and Levites—had intermarried with foreigners, and were following the detestable practices of the Canaanites. Worst of all, the leaders and officials had led the way. When Ezra heard this, he was appalled, and prayed:

> O my God, I am utterly ashamed; I blush to lift up my face to you. For our sins are piled higher than our heads, and our guilt has reached to the heavens. From the days of our ancestors until now, we have been steeped in sin. . . . But now we have been given a brief moment of grace, for the LORD our God has allowed a few of us to survive as a remnant. . . . And now, O our God, what can we say after all of this? For once again we have abandoned your commands! Your servants the prophets warned us when they said, "The land you are entering to possess is totally defiled by the detestable practices of the people living there. . . . Don't let your daughters marry their sons! Don't take their daughters as wives for your sons". . . . Now we are being punished because of our wickedness and our great guilt. But we have actually been punished far less than we deserve. . . . But even so, we are again breaking your commands and intermarrying with people who do these detestable things. . . . We come before you in our guilt as nothing but an escaped remnant, though in such a condition none of us can stand in your presence.
>
> EZRA 9:6–8, 10–15 NLT

Ezra, like Daniel before him, confessed on behalf of his people. While he wept and prayed, a large crowd gathered and wept with him. Then those who had sinned vowed to put away their pagan wives. Now these wives could have converted and become God's covenant people (Ruth 2:12; Esther 8:17). But those who refused were sent away.

Ezra said, "We have been given a brief moment of grace," but then lamented, "Once again we have abandoned your commands." God warns of the danger of abusing His grace: "[God] will speak peace unto his people, and to his saints: but let them not turn again to folly" (Psalm 85:8 KJV).

65. Prayer for Favor

In the palace at Susa, a Jew named Nehemiah was cupbearer
to the Persian king. One day his brother came from Judah, and
Nehemiah asked how the Jews there were doing. His brother
reported, "Those who survived the exile. . .are in great trouble
and disgrace. The wall of Jerusalem is broken down, and its gates
have been burned with fire" (Nehemiah 1:3 NIV).

When Nehemiah heard this, he fasted for several days. Then
he prayed: "LORD, the God of heaven, the great and awesome
God, who keeps his covenant of love with those who love him
and keep his commandments, let your ear be attentive and
your eyes open to hear the prayer your servant is praying before
you day and night for your servants, the people of Israel. . . .
Remember the instruction you gave. . .'If you are unfaithful, I
will scatter you among the nations, but if you return to me and
obey my commands, then even if your exiled people are at the
farthest horizon, I will gather them from there and bring them
to the place I have chosen as a dwelling for my Name.'. . . Lord,
let your ear be attentive to the prayer of this your servant and to
the prayer of your servants who delight in revering your name.
Give your servant success today by granting him favor in the
presence of this man" (Nehemiah 1:5–6, 8–9, 11 NIV). By "this
man" Nehemiah meant the Persian king.

The next time Nehemiah served the king, he explained that
his ancestral city was in ruins, so the king asked, "What is it you
want?" (Nehemiah 2:4 NIV). Nehemiah shot a quick prayer to
God then asked to go to Jerusalem to rebuild it. This pleased the
king, so Nehemiah asked for letters to the governors there to
provide him safe-conduct, and a letter to the keeper of the forests
to give him timber. The king granted all these requests.

Nehemiah had carefully thought through his petitions. But he didn't depend on his own cleverness to win the king's favor. He depended on God. Solomon had said, "The king's heart is in the hand of the LORD, like the rivers of water; He turns it wherever He wishes" (Proverbs 21:1 NKJV). Nehemiah quoted God's Word to Him, reminding Him of His promises, and God moved the king's heart in Nehemiah's favor.

66. Praying for Encouragement and Strength

Nehemiah led the rebuilding of Jerusalem's walls, but when the Horonite official Sanballat heard of it, he mocked them: "What are these feeble Jews doing? . . . Can they revive the stones from the dusty rubble even the burned ones?" (Nehemiah 4:2 NASB). Tobiah, a powerful Ammonite governor, joked, "If a fox should jump on it, he would break their stone wall down!" (Nehemiah 4:3 NASB).

So Nehemiah prayed, "Hear, O our God, how we are despised! Return their reproach on their own heads. . . . Do not forgive their iniquity and let not their sin be blotted out before You, for they have demoralized the builders" (Nehemiah 4:4–5 NASB).

Nehemiah and the Jews pressed on, and soon the whole wall was built to half its height because "the people had a mind to work" (Nehemiah 4:6 NASB). So the Jews' enemies sought to destroy their resolve. They conspired to attack the weary workers, but Nehemiah set a guard, and he and his men continually prayed.

But after a while they despaired. "The strength of the burden bearers is failing, yet there is much rubbish; and we ourselves are unable to rebuild the wall." Much of their depression was caused by their enemies' constant attrition: "They will not know or see until we come among them, kill them and put a stop to the work." And several Jews warned, "They will come up against us from every place where you may turn" (Nehemiah 4:10–12 NASB).

On top of it, Jewish so-called prophets gave warnings that Nehemiah was doomed to fail. He wrote, "All of them were trying to frighten us, thinking, 'They will become discouraged with the work and it will not be done.' But now, O God, strengthen my hands." He also prayed, "Remember, O my God, Tobiah and Sanballat according to these works of theirs, and also. . .the prophets who were trying to frighten me" (Nehemiah 6:9, 14 NASB).

Nehemiah had his eyes fixed on God and prayed nonstop, and God heard his prayers and strengthened the people—so much so that the entire city wall was rebuilt in only fifty-two days! What a difference the inspiration and power of God make in even ordinary manual labor! When their enemies saw this, they recognized that this work had been accomplished with the help of God.

67. Prayers That Upset the Lord

One day a man covered with leprosy came to Jesus, bowed low, and begged, "Lord, if you are willing, you can make me clean." Jesus reached out and touched him, saying, "I am willing. . . . Be clean!" Immediately he was healed (Luke 5:12–13 NIV).

Mark's Gospel gives additional details. In almost every Greek manuscript, the word *splangnistheis* ("feeling compassion") appears in Mark 1:41. Thus, most Bibles read that when the leper said, "If you are willing, you can make me clean," Jesus felt compassion. As the 1984 version of the NIV reads, "Filled with compassion, Jesus reached out his hand and touched the man." But in *one* Greek manuscript, Codex Bezae, the word *orgistheis* ("becoming angry") appears. Thus, the 2011 version of the NIV reads, "Jesus was indignant. He reached out his hand and touched the man."

It makes no difference to our understanding of Jesus' nature which word was original. We can understand Him having compassion on a poor leper (Matthew 14:14; 20:34). And Mark also shows Jesus becoming indignant on occasion (Mark 3:5; 10:14).

With such a difference between *orgistheis* and *splangnistheis*, how did this scribal error occur? Very likely, a Jewish Christian fluent in both Aramaic and Greek, when copying Mark's Gospel, would have realized that the underlying Aramaic word *ethra'em* ("he was enraged") is easily confused with *ethraham* ("he had pity"). Concluding that a translation error had been made, he changed the Greek word accordingly.

But all this may leave you wondering if God sometimes gets angry when you pray. Perhaps *displeased* is more accurate. The leper said, "If you are willing, you can make me clean." If Jesus did actually get upset, it was because the man doubted His willingness. We know from Hebrews 11:6 (NIV) that "without faith it is impossible to please God." So He *is* displeased with lack of faith.

Once, a father brought his son to Jesus' disciples but they couldn't heal him. Jesus said, "You unbelieving generation. . . . How long shall I put up with you?" (Mark 9:19 NIV). Then the father said, "If you can do anything, take pity on us and help us." Jesus replied sharply, " 'If you can'? . . . Everything is possible for one who believes" (Mark 9:22–23 NIV).

So yes, it does appear that some prayers upset God.

68. An Unexpected Answer

Jesus had only done one miracle in Galilee—turning water into wine in Cana—but when He was in Jerusalem at the Passover, "many believed in His name when they saw the signs which He did" (John 2:23 NKJV). Now He returned to Cana in Galilee. Thousands of returning pilgrims spread the news of His Jerusalem miracles throughout Galilee, and a nobleman of Capernaum heard. His son was dying of high fever, so he hurried to Cana, eighteen miles away. He tracked down Jesus at 1:00 p.m.

But when he asked Him to come heal his son, Jesus replied, "Unless you people see signs and wonders, you will by no means believe" (John 4:48 NKJV). But the nobleman had faith. He wasn't like many other Jews idly seeking signs. His heart brimming with emotion, he begged, "Sir, come down before my child dies!" (John 4:49 NKJV).

Jesus didn't wish to travel to Capernaum at that time—and there wasn't a need that He do so. He simply said, "Go your way; your son lives" (John 4:50 NKJV). The nobleman could have insisted that Jesus needed to be physically present to heal his son. After all, wasn't that how it was done? Instead, he believed Jesus and headed back to Capernaum. He didn't make it home that day, but that night he went to sleep trusting. The next morning he met his servants on the road, who told him that his son was cured.

When the nobleman asked what time he'd recovered, they replied, "Yesterday afternoon at one o'clock his fever suddenly disappeared!" (John 4:52 NLT). The nobleman realized that was the exact time that Jesus had said, "Your son lives," so he and his entire household became believers.

The nobleman didn't make a long petition. He first explained his need to Jesus then made a short, emotional request. But he had faith, so it was enough.

God doesn't always answer prayers the way we think He will. Naaman the Syrian, for example, became offended when Elisha didn't come out to meet him. He said, "I expected him to wave his hand over the leprosy and call on the name of the LORD his God and heal me!" (2 Kings 5:11 NLT). But Elisha gave him different instructions, and he obeyed them and was healed. God's answers are not always what we expect.

69. The Lord's Prayer

When Jesus' disciples asked, "Lord, teach us to pray," Jesus replied, "When you pray, say: Our Father in heaven, hallowed be Your name. Your kingdom come. Your will be done on earth as it is in heaven. Give us day by day our daily bread. And forgive us our sins, for we also forgive everyone who is indebted to us. And do not lead us into temptation, but deliver us from the evil one" (Luke 11:1–4 NKJV).

The Lord's Prayer, as it's often called, is the most famous prayer in the Bible. It's a model of simplicity, yet complete: a Christian praying this gives praise to God, prays for His will to be done (and, by extension, yields to God's will), prays for his or her physical needs, is reminded of the need for forgiveness, and requests protection from evil. This prayer is not only beautiful, but its brevity makes a powerful point: state your requests simply and clearly.

Now, because Jesus said, "When you pray, *say*"—then supplied the exact words—some people believe that this is exactly what He intended Christians to pray. So they memorize it and recite it word for word—sometimes several times in a row. But while repeating this prayer can be very enriching, it is actually meant as a model, not a magical mantra.

This is demonstrated by the fact that there isn't just one version of the Lord's Prayer. The wording in Luke is slightly different from the more frequently quoted version in Matthew 6:9–13. That's probably because Jesus taught this prayer on different occasion, and because the prayer's essence is more important than repeating it verbatim.

Also, when Jesus' disciples asked, "Lord, teach us to pray," in the Gospel of Luke, He first taught them the Lord's Prayer

(11:1–4); then He taught them the importance of persistent prayer (vv. 5–8); then He taught that God would answer sincere prayers (vv. 9–10); finally, He reinforced this by teaching that God answers because He isn't capricious, but good (vv. 11–13). In answer to the disciples' request, Jesus taught much more than just the Lord's Prayer.

Still, this brief but beloved prayer contains many spiritual riches. We do well to think deeply on what it says and means while we're praying it.

70. Say the Word and It's Done

One day Jesus went to Capernaum. At that time a local Roman centurion's slave was "paralyzed, dreadfully tormented," and near death (Matthew 8:6 NKJV). The centurion heard that Jesus had come back to Capernaum. Being responsible for crowd control, he had often watched Jesus surrounded by large crowds, performing astonishing healing miracles (Mark 1:32–34). So he knew that Jesus could heal.

But he was also aware that Jews were forbidden to enter Gentiles' houses or even associate with them (Acts 10:28). But since he had financed the building of their new synagogue, and since this was an emergency, he asked some Jewish elders to approach Jesus on his behalf. The elders earnestly petitioned Jesus: "If anyone deserves your help, he does. . .for he loves the Jewish people and even built a synagogue for us" (Luke 7:4–5 NLT).

So Jesus went with them. Meanwhile, the centurion, sensitive to Jewish scruples, thought hard of an alternate way of healing his servant. And he came up with the perfect solution.

Just before Jesus arrived at his house, the centurion sent some friends to say, "Lord, don't trouble yourself by coming to my home, for I am not worthy of such an honor. I am not even worthy to come and meet you. Just say the word from where you are, and my servant will be healed. I know this because I am under the authority of my superior officers, and I have authority over my soldiers. I only need to say, 'Go,' and they go, or 'Come,' and they come. And if I say to my slaves, 'Do this,' they do it" (Luke 7:6–8 NLT).

Turning to the crowd, Jesus said, "I tell you, I haven't seen faith like this in all Israel!" (Luke 7:9 NLT). And when the centurion's friends returned to his house, they found his slave completely healed.

The centurion had great faith, but this faith was built on practical everyday experience. He already knew that Jesus had healing power. So he took the principle of obedience in a military chain of command and applied it. He didn't need to be present to ensure that *his* orders were carried out, so logically, neither did Jesus. Like him, Jesus needed only to say the word and it was done.

71. Terrified, Panicked Prayers

Jesus had spent a long day ministering, and people were still arriving when evening came. He was worn out, so seeing the crowd around Him, He said, "Let us go over to the other side of the lake" (Luke 8:22 NASB). Jesus had a reason to go there, but He also needed to get some sleep. So, leaving the crowd, the disciples "took Him along with them in the boat, just as He was" (Mark 4:36 NASB)—totally exhausted.

As the boat launched out, Jesus collapsed on a cushion in the stern and was soon fast asleep. They sailed in the fading daylight, and other boats were with them. Some of the crowd were still following, intent on tapping into Jesus' power.

But some distance out a fierce gale of wind arose, huge waves were breaking over the boat, and it began filling up. They were all drenched. So was Jesus, but He was so spent that He didn't wake up.

The disciples came to Jesus, crying, "Master, Master, we are perishing!" (Luke 8:24 NASB). When He didn't wake up, they probably shook Him. Then they shouted, "Teacher, do You not care that we are perishing?" (Mark 4:38 NASB). Jesus awoke and asked, "Why are you afraid, you men of little faith?" (Matthew 8:26 NASB).

Wearily, He got up, rebuked the wind and commanded the surging waves, "Hush, be still" (Mark 4:39 NASB). Immediately the wind stopped and the waves subsided. It became perfectly calm.

The disciples were astonished, hardly able to believe the sudden transformation, so Jesus asked, "Where is your faith?" (Luke 8:25 NASB). When they remained speechless, He asked, "Why are you afraid? Do you still have no faith?" (Mark 4:40 NASB). The disciples had been afraid of the storm. Now they were afraid of Jesus. Wide-eyed, they said, "Who then is this, that He commands even the winds and the water, and they obey Him?" (Luke 8:25 NASB).

The disciples cried to Jesus in their great need, and the truth was, they were in real danger. But in their terror, they had completely abandoned their faith that God could act. Their prayers were panicked, desperate wails. Jesus was saying that *they* could have confidently prayed to their God themselves to calm the storm. They didn't need to wake Him up. But clearly they didn't have the faith for that.

72. Even Now You Can Act

Jesus crossed back over the Sea of Galilee to Capernaum, and a huge crowd gathered around Him. Then one of the rulers of the synagogue named Jairus pushed through the throng. He bowed at Jesus' feet and begged, "My little daughter lies at the point of death. Come and lay Your hands on her, that she may be healed, and she will live" (Mark 5:23 NKJV). So Jesus went with him, and the multitude followed.

As they walked, a woman suffering from a flow of blood stooped behind Jesus and touched the edge of His garment. He came to a sudden stop. The crowd stopped, too, though Jairus seems to have continued on a ways. When Jesus learned who had touched Him and why, He assured the woman that she had been made well.

But while Jesus was still speaking, messengers came from Jairus's house and told him, "Your daughter is dead. Why trouble the Teacher any further?" (Mark 5:35 NKJV). Jairus rushed back to where Jesus was standing and said, "My daughter has just died, but come and lay Your hand on her and she will live" (Matthew 9:18 NKJV).

Jairus still believed, but his faith was being severely tested, so Jesus said, "Do not be afraid; only believe" (Mark 5:36 NKJV).

When He came to the house, Jesus saw a tumult and women weeping and wailing loudly. Jesus shooed them all from the house and entered the room where the young girl lay. Only Peter, James, John, and the girl's parents accompanied Him. Then Jesus took her by the hand and said, "Little girl, I say to you, arise" (Mark 5:41 NKJV). Immediately she arose. Everyone was overcome with amazement, and the news of this miracle swept across the entire region.

Jairus petitioned Jesus *twice*—first when his daughter was dying and barely alive, and again after she had just died. He expressed faith in both prayers and never stopped believing that Jesus could heal his daughter.

Many people pray and trust God to act in difficult situations, but their faith fails when worse news comes and things suddenly look impossible. The messengers asked, "Why trouble the Teacher any further?" Some people think that when things get desperate, to *continue* praying is bothering the Lord for no reason. But God can not only do the difficult, He can do the impossible.

73. Touching Jesus

As Jesus went with Jairus to his house, a large crowd followed and pressed around Him, at times almost crushing Him. A woman was there who had experienced constant bleeding for twelve years. She had suffered a great deal under the care of many doctors and had spent all she had, yet only grew worse. So she came up behind Jesus in the crowd because she thought, "If I just touch his clothes, I will be healed" (Mark 5:28 NIV).

The second she touched His cloak her bleeding stopped and she felt in her body that she was healed from her suffering. Instantly Jesus knew that power had gone out from Him, so He turned and asked, "Who touched my clothes?" His disciples answered, "You see the people crowding against you. . .and yet you can ask, 'Who touched me?' " (Mark 5:30–31 NIV).

Jesus kept looking around to see who had done it. He insisted, "Someone touched me; I know that power has gone out from me" (Luke 8:46 NIV). Then the woman, realizing that she couldn't hide, came forward. She fell at his feet and, trembling with fear, told Him the whole truth. So Jesus said to her, "Daughter, your faith has healed you. Go in peace" (Luke 8:48 NIV).

This nameless woman had prayed a silent prayer. She didn't even speak her request. She only thought it. But she had faith in her heart, and when she made contact with Jesus, healing power flowed out of Him into her body. Christians today also need to touch Jesus, to make faith-filled contact with Him.

The woman knew that her bloody discharge made her ceremonially impure and that anyone who touched her became "unclean" (Leviticus 15:25–33). She was not allowed to touch anyone, either, so she merely brushed her fingers against the edge of Jesus' clothing. But because of her faith, that contact was enough.

The woman was embarrassed about her illness. She didn't want to admit what she needed healing from, but that's what she eventually had to do. Some Christians think that believers should enjoy perfect health all the time. So they're ashamed to confess when they get sick, because all their friends will think that they disobeyed God. But that doctrine isn't true. Sometimes sickness just happens. It's part of the fallen condition of the world.

74. Believe When You Pray

After Jesus healed Jairus's daughter, he headed for Peter's house nearby. But as He crossed the small city, two blind men followed Him, shouting, "Son of David, have mercy on us!" (Matthew 9:27 NLT). They wouldn't stop. Their request was simple, and they repeated it over and over again.

Some months later, Jesus encountered an almost identical situation in Jericho. Two blind men heard that He was coming their way and began shouting, "Lord, Son of David, have mercy on us!" The crowd ordered, "Be quiet!" But they were not deterred, shouting louder, "Lord, Son of David, have mercy on us!" (Matthew 20:30–31 NLT).

The two blind men in Capernaum were just as persistent. They boldly followed Jesus right into Peter's house. So He asked, "Do you believe I can make you see?" They replied, "Yes, Lord. . .we do." So He touched their eyes and said, "Because of your faith, it will happen" (Matthew 9:28–29 NLT). Then they received their sight.

They were overjoyed, but Jesus warned, "Don't tell anyone about this" (Matthew 9:30 NLT). However, they went out and spread his fame all over. Jesus had just given the same warning to Jairus and his wife, but too many other people there couldn't keep silent (Mark 5:43; Matthew 9:26).

The NLT has Jesus saying, "Because of your faith, it will happen." But in the NKJV, which is closer to the original Greek, He says, "According to your faith let it be to you." This leaves open the possibility that although they *claimed* to have faith, they might have lacked it. In other words, the onus was on them: they'd receive an answer to prayer in direct proportion to their faith. Fortunately, they had faith.

It was important that people had faith when coming to Jesus for help. When they lacked it, this limited Him. For example, in Nazareth "He could do no mighty work. . .except that He laid His hands on a few sick people and healed them. And He marveled because of their unbelief" (Mark 6:5–6 NKJV). In other cases, people confessed that they believed yet had doubts (Mark 9:23–24).

If you lack faith that God can answer your prayer, soak yourself in His Word and pray for Him to increase your faith (Luke 17:5). He will do it. "Faith comes by hearing, and hearing by the word of God" (Romans 10:17 NKJV).

75. Lord, Save Me!

After multiplying bread and fishes for a multitude, Jesus instructed the twelve apostles to get into a boat and cross the lake while He stayed behind and sent the crowds away. Then He went up the mountain to pray. When darkness settled over Galilee, the boat was a long distance from the land, battered by waves and fighting headwinds.

About three o'clock in the morning Jesus came, walking on the dark, surging sea. When the disciples saw Him atop the storm-tossed waves, they were terrified and shouted, "It is a ghost!" and cried out in fear. But Jesus said, "Take courage, it is I; do not be afraid" (Matthew 14:26–27 NASB).

Peter, impetuous as always, blurted out, "Lord, if it is You, command me to come to You on the water" (Matthew 14:28 NASB). It's hard to imagine what motivated this request, but Jesus honored it, saying, "Come!" So Peter got out of the boat and walked on the heaving waters. But some ways out he took his eyes off Jesus and became frightened by the wind and waves. Instantly he began to sink. He cried, "Lord, save me!" (Matthew 14:30 NASB), so Jesus grabbed him and kept him on the surface.

Then He asked, "You of little faith, why did you doubt?" (Matthew 14:31 NASB).

Peter had been filled with a sudden surge of faith and stepped out on the waters. Great faith for unusual acts often comes suddenly—but it can be just as suddenly lost, as Peter learned. "We walk by faith, not by sight" (2 Corinthians 5:7 NKJV). Fear and doubt short-circuited his faith, and he could no longer do the miraculous.

Jesus asked, "Why did you doubt?" Can we actually choose to have faith—or to *not* have it? Yes, people do this all the time.

Jesus talked about those who "when they hear, receive the word with joy. . .which *for a while believe*, and in time of temptation fall away" (Luke 8:13 KJV, emphasis added). Did what tempted them convince them that their faith was wrong? No. But after they gave into temptation, they *chose* to discard their faith and stop believing. And many people believe for miracles in fair weather but allow themselves to lose their confidence when trouble hits.

But the good news is that you can make a conscious decision to be willing to believe—and God will honor that.

76. A Persistent Request

Leaving Galilee, Jesus and His disciples traveled north to the coast of Phoenicia, in the region of the cities of Tyre and Sidon. Things were dangerous in Galilee, and since there was a large Jewish population up north, Jesus went there.

The Phoenicians were Canaanites, and the Jews had nothing to do with Gentiles—let alone Canaanites. But a Canaanite woman came to the house where Jesus was staying: "Lord, Son of David, have mercy on me! My daughter is demon-possessed and suffering terribly" (Matthew 15:22 NIV). *Son of David* was a title for the Messiah, so this woman believed that Jesus was the promised Savior.

Jesus heard her but didn't answer, so His disciples urged Him, "Send her away, for she keeps crying out after us." Jesus turned to the woman and explained, "I was sent only to the lost sheep of Israel" (Matthew 15:23–24 NIV).

Desperate, trusting in His goodness, the woman knelt before Him, insisting, "Lord, help me!" (Matthew 15:25 NIV).

Jesus replied, "First let the children eat all they want. . .it is not right to take the children's bread and toss it to the dogs" (Mark 7:27 NIV). Jews often referred to Gentiles as dogs, and it wasn't a compliment, but the woman used Jesus' illustration to argue for His help: "Yes it is, Lord. . . . Even the dogs eat the crumbs that fall from their master's table" (Matthew 15:27 NIV).

Jesus said, " 'Woman, you have great faith! Your request is granted.' And her daughter was healed at that moment" (Matthew 15:28 NIV).

God counted even Canaanites righteous if they had faith in God. Consider Rahab, one of Jesus' ancestors (Matthew 1:5; Hebrews 11:31). But God had sent Jesus to the Jews. After His

chosen people had heard the message, it could go to the Gentiles
. . .but not before. So Jesus ignored the woman. But the woman's
great humility and faith bumped her forward in the line.

The woman's dogged persistence also helped her get an
answer. She knew that Jesus had the power to help her, and
since He was her only hope, she refused to take no for an
answer. Even if you feel unworthy, cast yourself on God's mercy
and ask Him to help you. If others tell you it's not possible for
your prayers to be answered, keep praying.

77. Help My Unbelief

Jesus was atop a mountain with Peter, James, and John, and when they came down, they saw a crowd gathered and scribes arguing with Jesus' disciples. Jesus asked, "What is all this arguing about?" A man said, "Teacher, I brought my son so you could heal him. He is possessed by an evil spirit that won't let him talk. And whenever this spirit seizes him, it throws him violently to the ground. Then he foams at the mouth and grinds his teeth and becomes rigid. So I asked your disciples to cast out the evil spirit, but they couldn't do it" (Mark 9:16–18 NLT).

Jesus said, "You faithless people! How long must I be with you? How long must I put up with you? Bring the boy to me." So they brought him. Then the evil spirit "threw the child into a violent convulsion, and he fell to the ground, writhing and foaming at the mouth." "How long has this been happening?" Jesus asked (Mark 9:19–21 NLT).

The boy's father replied, "Since he was a little boy. . . . Have mercy on us and help us, if you can" (Mark 9:21–22 NLT).

"What do you mean, 'If I can'?" Jesus responded. "Anything is possible if a person believes." The father cried out, "I do believe, but help me overcome my unbelief!" So Jesus rebuked the evil spirit: "I command you to come out of this child and never enter him again!" (Mark 9:23–25 NLT). The spirit screamed, threw the boy into a violent convulsion, and left him. Then Jesus helped him to his feet.

Afterward, Jesus' disciples asked Him, "Why couldn't we cast out that demon?" Jesus gave two answers. First, He told them, "You don't have enough faith" (Matthew 17:19–20 NLT). When Jesus said, "You faithless people!" this included not only the boy's father, but His own disciples. They *should* have been able to cast out the evil spirit. Jesus had already given them power for that (Matthew 10:8; Luke 10:17–19).

Jesus' second answer was, "This kind can be cast out only by prayer" (Mark 9:29 NLT). In other words, the disciples needed to get militant about it, not only for a short while and then give up, but to persevere in prayer. The NKJV says, "This kind can come out by nothing but prayer and fasting." The idea is to concentrate in prayer for some time.

78. A Presumptuous Request

When Jesus and His apostles were making their way to Jerusalem, He promised, "When the Son of Man sits on his glorious throne, you who have followed me will also sit on twelve thrones, judging the twelve tribes of Israel" (Matthew 19:28 niv).

This was a fantastic promise, but James and John, who were brothers, wanted the very *best* thrones. They figured that they deserved them. After all, besides Peter, they were Jesus' closest disciples. So they talked it over with their mother, and when everyone stopped to rest, they came to Jesus, just out of earshot of the other apostles, and said, "Teacher, we want You to do for us whatever we ask" (Mark 10:35 nkjv).

He asked, "What do you want Me to do for you?" (Mark 10:36 nkjv).

They answered, "Grant us that we may sit, one on Your right hand and the other on Your left, in Your glory" (Mark 10:37 nkjv).

Jesus responded, "You do not know what you ask. . . . To sit on My right hand and on My left is not Mine to give, but it is for those for whom it is prepared" (Mark 10:38, 40 nkjv).

When the other apostles got wind of what James and John had requested, they were very upset. But Jesus called them over and explained, "Those who are considered rulers over the Gentiles lord it over them, and their great ones exercise authority over them. Yet it shall not be so among you; but. . .whoever of you desires to be first shall be slave of all" (Mark 10:42–44 nkjv). It's not wrong to desire to be first in God's kingdom. Just understand that this means putting your own desires last and living your entire life serving others.

Like James and John, we often have a self-centered idea of

greatness. The Bible says that "if we ask anything according to His will. . .we have the petitions that we have asked of Him" (1 John 5:14–15 NKJV), but many things that we ask for are *not* God's will. To them Jesus says, "You do not know what you ask." Far too often we pray to the Lord, "We want You to do for us whatever we ask." In other words, "Be our personal genie and grant our every wish and heart's desire." But God's kingdom isn't set up that way, and He usually doesn't answer such prayers.

79. Impossible Prayer Requests

Jesus said, "All things are possible to him who believes" (Mark 9:23 NASB). As long as there's life, there's hope, so we should never give up believing that God can turn difficult situations around. But *after* this life is over, *all* things are no longer possible.

Jesus told a story about a rich man who dressed in fine clothing, feasted, and lived happily every day. A man named Lazarus, covered with sores, begged at his gate but often went hungry. Then Lazarus died and was carried by the angels to Abraham's bosom. The rich man also died—but went to Hades. He looked up and saw Abraham and Lazarus far away. So he shouted, "Father Abraham, have mercy on me, and send Lazarus so that he may dip the tip of his finger in water and cool off my tongue, for I am in agony in this flame" (Luke 16:24 NASB).

But Abraham gave two reasons why that wasn't possible. He said, "Remember that during your life you received your good things, and likewise Lazarus bad things; but now he is being comforted here, and you are in agony. And besides all this, between us and you there is a great chasm fixed, so that those who wish to come over from here to you will not be able, and that none may cross over from there to us" (Luke 16:25–26 NASB).

The rich man then begged Abraham to send Lazarus to his brothers to warn them, but again Abraham said no. When the rich man argued that they'd believe if they saw someone raised from the dead, again Abraham said no. Many things you might want to pray for are no longer possible after death.

Many silly or ridiculous prayer requests aren't possible even in this life. For example, you could pray to continually win the lottery, or pray that no one in the world would be sick, or pray for all wars to end now. While these are obviously irrational, a surprising number of modern prayer requests border on being unreasonable or ridiculous.

God has not only fixed great chasms in the spiritual realm but has set up laws in this physical world that render certain requests impossible. So it's best not to waste your time praying for those things.

80. Pray and Never Give Up

One day Jesus told His disciples a story to teach them how to pray. Like most people, they became discouraged or bewildered when God seemed to ignore their oft-repeated prayers. So Jesus told a parable to show that they should pray and *keep on* praying and never give up.

"There was a judge in a certain city," he said, "who neither feared God nor cared about people. A widow of that city came to him repeatedly, saying, 'Give me justice in this dispute with my enemy.' The judge ignored her for a while, but finally he said to himself, 'I don't fear God or care about people, but this woman is driving me crazy. I'm going to see that she gets justice, because she is wearing me out with her constant requests!' " (Luke 18:2–5 NLT).

Then Jesus said, "Learn a lesson from this unjust judge. Even he rendered a just decision in the end. So don't you think God will surely give justice to his chosen people who cry out to him day and night? Will he keep putting them off? I tell you, he will grant justice to them quickly! But when the Son of Man returns, how many will he find on the earth who have faith?" (Luke 18:6–8 NLT).

Some people think that Jesus was saying that His Father was just like the unjust judge—unwilling to answer the pitiful prayers of desperate people, unless they pester Him to death. But to think that is to miss the plain point of the parable. Jesus was saying that if even an unjust judge could be finally moved to act, *how much more* would their loving heavenly Father?

Jesus made a similar statement to a crowd of men and women: "If you then, being evil, know how to give good gifts to your children, how much more will your Father who is in heaven give good things to those who ask Him!" (Matthew 7:11 NKJV). Indeed! Much more!

You may be crying out to God but feel as if He's putting you off or turning a deaf ear to you. But *continue* crying out. "Pray and never give up" (Luke 18:1 NLT). There will be times—perhaps many times—when you will need to pray repeatedly for the same thing. So don't get discouraged. Be persistent.

81. Believing and Thanking God

On His final trip south to Jerusalem, Jesus and the apostles traveled along the border between Samaria and Galilee. As Jesus was going into a village, ten leprous men met Him. They stood at a distance—as the Mosaic Law required they do—and called out in a loud voice, "Jesus, Master, have pity on us!" When He saw their disease, Jesus called back, "Go, show yourselves to the priests" (Luke 17:13–14 NIV). This was the required procedure after someone had been cleansed of leprosy (Leviticus 13:2–3; 14:2–32).

The ten lepers immediately headed off to see the priests, and "as they went, they were cleansed" (Luke 17:14 NIV).

One of them, when he saw he was healed, came running back, praising God in a loud voice. He threw himself at Jesus' feet and thanked Him, and he was a Samaritan. Jesus asked, "Were not all ten cleansed? Where are the other nine? Has no one returned to give praise to God except this foreigner? . . . Rise and go; your faith has made you well" (Luke 17:17–19 NIV).

There are three lessons in this story: the first one is that "your Father knows what you need before you ask him" (Matthew 6:8 NIV). The lepers didn't even need to say, "Heal us of our leprosy!" All they needed to do was cry out, "Jesus, Master, have pity on us!" Jesus could see what their need was.

Second, God expects us to act out our faith. Jesus sent the lepers to the priests, and "*as they went*, they were cleansed" (emphasis added). Their faith made them well, and they proved that they had faith by heading to the priests while they still had leprosy. If they had simply stood there checking their bodies and waiting to be healed before they went, they may not have been healed.

The third lesson is that you must be thankful to God

when He answers your prayers. Expressing gratitude to human benefactors is common courtesy, and God expects no less. A number of people who have experienced miraculous healing or some other answer to prayer have later reported losing this blessing—often as a result of continuing to sin, or not valuing and being grateful for the miracle (John 5:14).

82. Pray Even Now

One day a messenger arrived from Bethany bringing Jesus an urgent message: Lazarus, the brother of Mary and Martha, was very sick. But after hearing the news, Jesus stayed two more days where He was. Finally, He announced that it was time to go to Judea. When they arrived, Lazarus had already been dead and in the tomb four days.

As soon as she heard that Jesus had come, Martha went out to meet Him, but Mary remained in the house. Martha said to Jesus, "Lord, if You had been here, my brother would not have died. But even now I know that whatever You ask of God, God will give You" (John 11:21–22 NKJV). This demonstrated tremendous faith, because—as Martha later pointed out— Lazarus's body had already begun to decompose.

Then Martha called Mary, and she came, followed by many Jews from nearby Jerusalem who were mourning with the sisters. When Jesus saw Mary and the Jews weeping, He groaned and asked, "Where have you laid him?" (John 11:34 NKJV). Then they took him to the tomb. It was a cave, and a stone lay over it. Jesus commanded, "Take away the stone" (John 11:39 NKJV). So they did.

Then Jesus looked up and prayed, "Father, I thank You that You have heard Me. And I know that You always hear Me, but because of the people who are standing by I said this, that they may believe that You sent Me." Then He shouted, "Lazarus, come forth!" And the dead man came out covered with graveclothes. Jesus said, "Loose him, and let him go" (John 11:41–44 NKJV).

So often it seems that God waits till the last possible moment to answer desperate prayers. And just as often, a critical deadline passes *without* an answer. The end of the month arrives and you still don't have your rent money. You pray for a sick child, but she doesn't improve. At times like that, you need the faith of Martha to say, "But *even now* I know that whatever You ask of God, God will give You."

It's not necessarily the end. . .even though it may seem that way. Jesus is always interceding for you before God's throne (Romans 8:34), and God can do the impossible. He may not answer how you hoped or expected He would, but He can answer.

83. The Pharisee and the Tax Collector

Some people in Jesus' day were proud of their righteousness and looked down on others who they felt weren't very holy. . .and this attitude permeated their prayers.

One day Jesus told a parable about two men. The first was a Pharisee (which comes from a word meaning "separated, set apart"). They were renowned for their scrupulous efforts to obey the letter of the Law and live a holy life. The second man was a tax collector. They were considered sinners because they associated with "unclean" Gentiles and often cheated their fellow Jews.

Yet Jesus taught: "Two men went up to the temple to pray, one a Pharisee and the other a tax collector. The Pharisee stood by himself and prayed: 'God, I thank you that I am not like other people—robbers, evildoers, adulterers—or even like this tax collector. I fast twice a week and give a tenth of all I get.' But the tax collector stood at a distance. He would not even look up to heaven, but beat his breast and said, 'God, have mercy on me, a sinner' " (Luke 18:10–13 NIV).

Jesus said, "I tell you that this man, rather than the other, went home justified before God. For all those who exalt themselves will be humbled, and those who humble themselves will be exalted" (Luke 18:14 NIV). The humble are more open to receiving salvation. Jesus told the religious leaders, "Truly I tell you, the tax collectors and the prostitutes are entering the kingdom of God ahead of you" (Matthew 21:31 NIV).

The Pharisee was confident of his own goodness and, to keep himself holy and uncontaminated, had no contact with *sinners*. If he touched a less pious Jew in the marketplace, he'd hurry home to wash his hands. His attitude was this: "Stand by thyself, come not near to me; for I am holier than thou" (Isaiah 65:5 KJV). This is why the Pharisee "stood by himself and prayed." And his prayer? It was a proud oratory, not a sincere, heartfelt cry to God. Small wonder God ignored him.

The tax collector, on the other hand, had no proud illusions. He *knew* that he was a sinner who had no righteousness to boast about, nor any hope apart from the mercy of God. His prayer came from a humble, contrite heart—and God heard him.

84. Refuse to Stop Crying Out

As Jesus and His disciples left Jericho, a large crowd followed them. A blind man named Bartimaeus was sitting beside the road, just outside the city gates. With him was another blind beggar.

When Bartimaeus heard that Jesus was passing by, he began to shout, "Jesus, Son of David, have mercy on me!" Several people scolded, "Be quiet!" but he just shouted louder, "Son of David, have mercy on me!" Jesus finally heard him, stopped, and said, "Tell him to come here." So the crowd called him. "Cheer up," they said. "Come on, he's calling you!" (Mark 10:47–49 NLT). Bartimaeus rose and made his way to Jesus. The other blind man followed.

"What do you want me to do for you?" Jesus asked. "My Rabbi," Bartimaeus said, "I want to see!" The other blind man echoed this plea. Jesus touched their eyes and said, "Go, for your faith has healed you." Instantly both men could see (Mark 10:51–52 NLT; see also Matthew 20:29–34).

This is a powerful lesson in persistence. With so many people ordering them to be quiet and not make a scene, the blind men could have given up. But they persisted, calling out again and again, getting louder all the time.

Jesus once taught a parable about a man whose friend arrived at midnight, but he had nothing to serve him. He banged on a friend's door, waking him up, and asked to borrow some bread. The man insisted he couldn't get up, but Jesus said, "I tell you this. . .if you keep knocking long enough, he will get up and give you whatever you need because of your shameless persistence. And so I tell you, keep on asking, and you will receive what you ask for" (Luke 11:8–9 NLT).

The two blind men had "shameless persistence." They were creating a disturbance and refused to be shamed into shutting up. The crowd thought that Jesus was ignoring them and wanted the beggars to politely accept His decision. But Jesus hadn't heard them over the noise of the crowd until they raised a real ruckus.

The crowd was enjoying promenading with a celebrity, basking in His presence. They had their program and didn't want any disruptions—least of all from two ragged beggars. But Jesus always had time for the downtrodden and despised.

85. When God Thunders

Six days before the Passover, Jesus and His disciples went to Jerusalem. The time had finally arrived for Jesus to be arrested and crucified, and He felt deep grief. He prayed, "Now My soul is troubled, and what shall I say? 'Father, save Me from this hour'? But for this purpose I came to this hour. Father, glorify Your name" (John 12:27–28 NKJV).

"Then a voice came from heaven, saying, 'I have both glorified it and will glorify it again.'. . . The people who stood by and heard it said that it had thundered. Others said, 'An angel has spoken to Him' " (John 12:28–29 NKJV). Jesus heard God's answer clearly, but others were not as sensitive and heard Him with varying clarity.

Then Jesus said, "This voice did not come because of Me, but for your sake." He added, "Now is the judgment of this world; now the ruler of this world will be cast out. And I, if I am lifted up from the earth, will draw all peoples to Myself" (John 12:30–32 NKJV). He was talking about the kind of death He would soon die.

Jesus had admitted, "My soul is troubled, and what shall I say?" When torn and uncertain, He simply prayed, "Father, glorify Your name." This echoes the Lord's Prayer: "Hallowed be Your name. . . . Your will be done" (Matthew 6:9–10 NKJV). When the way was darkest, Jesus prayed for His Father to be glorified by His will being done—despite the pain it caused Jesus.

At times you, too, won't know what to pray. You may have become convinced that a certain course of action is God's will, yet as it becomes clearer how much loss and pain this might entail, you question yourself. Can you still surrender to God's will? At times like this, Peter advised, "Let those who suffer according to the will of God commit their souls to Him in doing good, as to a faithful Creator" (1 Peter 4:19 NKJV).

God may or may not thunder in approval of your sacrifice, but even if He remains silent, He will "grant you, according to the riches of His glory, to be strengthened with might through His Spirit in the inner man" (Ephesians 3:16 NKJV). He will steel your resolve and give you the grace to suffer for His name.

86. Jesus' Prayer for Unity

In John 17, just before His death, Jesus prayed:

Father, the hour has come; glorify Your Son, that the Son may glorify You. . .that to all whom You have given Him, He may give eternal life. This is eternal life, that they may know You, the only true God, and Jesus Christ whom You have sent. . . . Father, glorify Me together with Yourself, with the glory which I had with You before the world was. I have manifested Your name to the men whom You gave Me out of the world; they were Yours and You gave them to Me. . . . Holy Father, keep them in Your name, the name which You have given Me, that they may be one even as We are. While I was with them, I was keeping them in Your name which You have given Me; and I guarded them. . . . I do not ask on behalf of these alone, but for those also who believe in Me through their word; that they may all be one; even as You, Father, are in Me and I in You, that they also may be in Us. . .that they may be one, just as We are one; I in them and You in Me, that they may be perfected in unity.

JOHN 17:1–6, 11–12, 20–23 NASB

Many Christians are enthralled by this prayer's great beauty but wonder if it actually applies to everyday reality. After all, how much are they actually one with Jesus and God? But this prayer accurately describes our union, since "if anyone does *not* have the Spirit of Christ, he is not His." But "he who *is* joined to the Lord is *one spirit* with Him" (Romans 8:9; 1 Corinthians 6:17 NKJV, emphasis added).

We are also one with other believers in the sense that we are one body, of whom Christ is the head (1 Corinthians 12:12–27). "So it is with Christ's body. We are many parts of one body, and we all belong to each other" (Romans 12:5 NLT).

But apart from describing a mystical spiritual union with Christ or other believers, Jesus was praying that we would be one in mind and heart by being in agreement with the will of God and living in love and harmony with one another.

87. Yielding to God's Will

When Jesus took His disciples to Gethsemane, He left them in the lower garden while He went higher up. He took Peter, James, and John with Him, instructing them, "Stay here and keep watch with me." Then, going a little farther, He prayed desperately, "My Father, if it is possible, may this cup be taken from me. Yet not as I will, but as you will" (Matthew 26:38–39 NIV).

After praying for some time, He returned to His disciples and found them sleeping. He went away again and prayed, "My Father, if it is not possible for this cup to be taken away unless I drink it, may your will be done" (Matthew 26:42 NIV).

When Jesus returned, He found them sleeping once more. So he left them and prayed the third time, saying the same words.

An angel appeared and strengthened Him. And being in anguish, He prayed more earnestly, and his sweat was "like great drops of blood falling to the ground" (Luke 22:44 NKJV). Going back to the disciples, He found them asleep again. Jesus announced, "Look, the hour has come, and the Son of Man is delivered into the hands of sinners" (Matthew 26:45 NIV). At that moment, Judas arrived with a mob.

Jesus completely yielded to His Father's will, however painful it was. Jesus "offered up prayers and supplications, with vehement cries and tears to Him who was able to save Him from death, and was heard because of His godly fear" (Hebrews 5:7 NKJV). Not only was his sweat "like great drops of blood," but Jesus wept with "vehement cries."

God was *able* to save Jesus from being crucified, and Jesus asked Him, if possible, to do precisely that—but then prayed, "Yet not as I will, but as you will." As He explained to Peter, "Do you think I cannot call on my Father, and he will at once put at my disposal more than twelve legions of angels? But how then would the Scriptures be fulfilled that say it must happen in this way?" (Matthew 26:53–54 NIV).

Sometimes you, too, will be asked to make painful sacrifices, and though you could get out of them if you really wanted to, God will bless you for yielding to His will.

88. A Prayer of Forgiveness

Jesus said, "Love your enemies! Pray for those who persecute you!" (Matthew 5:44 NLT).

Since Jesus advised people to pray for those who hated and harmed them, it comes as no surprise that He prayed for God to forgive His own executioners—while they were crucifying Him. "When they came to the place called The Skull, there they crucified Him and the criminals, one on the right and the other on the left. But Jesus was saying, 'Father, forgive them; for they do not know what they are doing' " (Luke 23:33–34 NASB).

You may think that Jesus could forgive them because He was the perfect Son of God, and He knew, after all, that it was God's will that He die on the cross. If so, you might assume that you'll be excused for not being able to love your enemies, and not forgive them. But Jesus gave a command then set an example to follow. And Christians like Stephen followed it. As he was dying, he forgave those who stoned him, praying, "Lord, don't charge them with this sin!" (Acts 7:60 NLT).

You need to pray for and forgive others for two reasons. The first reason is that it brings peace and healing to your own soul. It draws you close to God's heart and ensures that you'll be forgiven as well. The opposite is also true. Jesus said, "If you do not forgive others their sins, your Father will not forgive your sins" (Matthew 6:15 NIV).

And second, if you forgive others, God Himself forgives them for those particular sins and opens their eyes to His love and grace (John 20:23). If you forgive them, you then begin to pray for God to do good to them, beginning with their need for salvation. Jesus prayed for the Romans at the cross, and God caused faith to rise in their hearts. "So when the centurion and those with him, who were guarding Jesus, saw the earthquake and the things that had happened, they feared greatly, saying, 'Truly this was the Son of God!' " (Matthew 27:54 NKJV). Mark 15:39 adds that when the centurion heard the words Jesus spoke, he believed.

Prayers of forgiveness are some of the most difficult prayers you can possibly pray, but also some of the most important, because they can have such powerful results!

89. Jesus' Final Prayers

In His final moments on the cross, Jesus cried out four times, and while two of these utterances were prophetic statements, the other two were prayers to His Father. So what was in Jesus' heart during His final moments of suffering?

About 3:00 p.m., Jesus cried out with a loud voice, "Eli, Eli, lama sabachthani?" which means, "My God, My God, why have You forsaken Me?" (Matthew 27:46 NASB). When He took on the sin of the world (Isaiah 53:6; 2 Corinthians 5:21), Jesus momentarily felt as if His Father had abandoned Him. He was also quoting Psalm 22:1 to draw attention to the fact that the prophecies regarding His crucifixion were being fulfilled (Psalm 22:7–8, 14–18).

After this, knowing that He had accomplished all things, Jesus choked out, "I am thirsty" (John 19:28 NASB). A jar of sour wine (vinegar) was standing there, so they put a sponge full of it on a reed and brought it to His mouth. This fulfilled the Scripture, "For my thirst they gave me vinegar to drink" (Psalm 69:21 NASB).

When Jesus had received it, He said, "It is finished!" (John 19:30 NASB). He had done everything His Father had sent Him to do.

Then Jesus cried out with a loud voice, quoting Psalm 31:5, "Father, into Your hands I commit My spirit" (Luke 23:46 NASB). Then He bowed His head and gave up His spirit. Instantly, there was an earthquake and the veil of the temple was torn from top to bottom. When the centurion, who was standing there, heard Him and saw these things, he said, "Truly this man was the Son of God!" (Mark 15:39 NASB).

Some people focus on Jesus' cry, "Why have You forsaken

Me?" and claim that He died in despair, utterly separated from God, and on His way to a burning hell to suffer torment there. This wasn't the case. Jesus' next words—"It is finished"—show that having shed His life's blood, He had already done *everything* necessary to secure our salvation.

And Jesus' prayer, "Father, into Your hands I commit My spirit," showed His trust that He was headed to heaven. As He'd promised the repentant thief, "Truly I say to you, today you shall be with Me in Paradise" (Luke 23:43 NASB).

90. Praying and Casting Lots

After Jesus ascended from the Mount of Olives into heaven, the eleven apostles went into Jerusalem, accompanied by many other disciples, both men and women. Together all 120 of them assembled in a large room. "These all continued with one accord in prayer and supplication" (Acts 1:14 NKJV), praying nonstop for ten days.

Then Peter stood up and announced that although the prophecy had to be fulfilled that Judas would betray Jesus (Psalm 41:9), there was another prophecy that stated that someone should replace him: "Let another take his office" (Psalm 109:8 NKJV).

Almost everyone present had seen Jesus after His resurrection, a major prerequisite to being an apostle (1 Corinthians 9:1). As Peter explained, "One of these must become a witness with us of His resurrection" (Acts 1:22 NKJV). But there were other considerations as well: he had to have followed Jesus and witnessed His teachings and deeds during His entire ministry, from His baptism until His ascension. And an apostle had to do miracles and wonders (2 Corinthians 12:12).

Only two men fit all these qualifications: Joseph and Matthias. So the apostles prayed, "You, O Lord, who know the hearts of all, show which of these two You have chosen to take part in this ministry and apostleship from which Judas by transgression fell" (Acts 1:24–25 NKJV). Then they cast lots and the lot fell on Matthias. So he became the new twelfth apostle.

The exact nature of lots is unknown. They could have been flat, coin-like stones, some type of dice, or sticks of differing lengths. God's people often "cast lots. . .before the LORD" (Joshua 18:10 NKJV) in the Old Testament, and the way the lots fell was considered to be divinely guided: "The lot is cast. . .its every decision is from the LORD" (Proverbs 16:33 NKJV). Peter would have been familiar with these passages.

Some people insist that casting lots (usually flipping a coin) is still a valid way to determine God's will. However, even pagans cast lots to make decisions (Esther 3:7; Matthew 27:35), so other Christians contend that with the coming of God's Spirit to guide us, this former method was phased out—and shouldn't even have been used in Acts 1. They contend that *Paul* was God's choice for the twelfth apostle, but he wasn't present in the upper room.

91. Praying for Boldness

Just before ascending to heaven, Jesus had told His disciples, "You will receive power when the Holy Spirit comes on you; and you will be my witnesses" (Acts 1:8 NIV). And this is what happened at Pentecost. The believers were baptized with the Spirit and boldly proclaimed the message of Jesus' death and resurrection.

Later Peter and John were arrested for healing a lame man and preaching the Gospel. The religious leaders commanded them not to teach in the name of Jesus. When Peter and John refused to comply, their enemies threatened them further then released them. After they returned to the other disciples and reported what had happened, the believers cried out in prayer:

"Sovereign Lord. . .you made the heavens and the earth. . . . You spoke by the Holy Spirit through the mouth of your servant, our father David: 'Why do the nations rage and the peoples plot in vain? The kings of the earth rise up and the rulers band together against the Lord and against his anointed one.' Indeed Herod and Pontius Pilate met together with the Gentiles and the people of Israel in this city to conspire against your holy servant Jesus. . . . Lord, consider their threats and enable your servants to speak your word with great boldness. Stretch out your hand to heal and perform signs and wonders through the name of your holy servant Jesus" (Acts 4:24–27, 29–30 NIV).

After they had prayed, the place where they were meeting was physically shaken, and they were all filled with the Holy Spirit and spoke the word of God boldly.

Note the pattern in their prayer: the disciples first quoted the scripture to God—in this case, Psalm 2:1–2. They likely also quoted God's promised *response* to the officials' enraged plots: "The One enthroned in heaven laughs; the Lord scoffs at them. He rebukes them in his anger" (Psalm 2:4–5 NIV).

The religious rulers and the political rulers seemed to have all the power, but the disciples knew that *God* was actually ruler over all. That's why they prayed, "Sovereign Lord. . .you made the heavens and the earth." The rulers didn't have the power they thought they did. They merely did "what [God's] *power* and *will* had decided beforehand should happen" (Acts 4:28 NIV, emphasis added). God is still that powerful today.

92. What Shall I Do, Lord?

After Stephen's murder, Saul went to the high priest and asked for letters of authority to the synagogues at Damascus so that he could arrest Christians there and bring them to Jerusalem. But as he was approaching Damascus, a bright light from heaven flashed around him, and he fell to the ground.

Then Saul heard a voice asking, "Saul, Saul, why are you persecuting Me? It is hard for you to kick against the goads" (Acts 26:14 NASB). Jesus was trying to convict Saul like a farmer prodding an ox with a goad, but Saul, like a stubborn ox, was kicking back.

Saul asked, "Who are You, Lord?" He said, "I am Jesus whom you are persecuting" (Acts 9:5 NASB).

"What shall I do, Lord?" Saul asked. Jesus said, "Get up and go on into Damascus, and there you will be told of all that has been appointed for you to do" (Acts 22:10 NASB).

Then He added, "For this purpose I have appeared to you, to appoint you a minister and a witness not only to the things which you have seen, but also to the things in which I will appear to you. . .to open their eyes so that they may turn from darkness to light and from the dominion of Satan to God, that they may receive forgiveness of sins and an inheritance among those who have been sanctified by faith in Me" (Acts 26:16, 18 NASB).

The men traveling with Saul were speechless, hearing the sound of a voice but unable to make out the words. And they saw the light but couldn't distinguish a form. But Saul saw and heard the Son of God in all His glory and immediately addressed Him as "Lord." No human reasoning or logic had been able to convince Saul, but encountering the risen Savior, he went instantly from an enraged enemy to a meek follower, praying for Jesus to show him what to do.

Saul had without doubt been praying to God before that, but they were the prayers of a hateful, self-willed man, not someone who had a loving relationship with God and was yielded to His will. But from the moment he encountered the Lord, Saul's prayers came from a humble, obedient heart. Rather than asking Him to sanction his agenda, Saul prayed, "What shall I do, Lord?"

93. Question and Answer

There was a disciple at Damascus named Ananias, and the Lord called out to him in a vision, "Ananias."

He answered, "Here I am, Lord."

The Lord said, "Arise and go to the street called Straight, and inquire at the house of Judas for one called Saul of Tarsus, for behold, he is praying. And in a vision he has seen a man named Ananias coming in and putting his hand on him, so that he might receive his sight" (Acts 9:11–12 NKJV).

Ananias was shocked, and prayed, "Lord, I have heard from many about this man, how much harm he has done to Your saints in Jerusalem. And here he has authority from the chief priests to bind all who call on Your name" (Acts 9:13–14 NKJV).

The Lord reassured Ananias, "Go, for he is a chosen vessel of Mine to bear My name before Gentiles, kings, and the children of Israel. For I will show him how many things he must suffer for My name's sake" (Acts 9:15–16 NKJV).

So Ananias went to Straight Street, entered the house, and laying his hands on him, said, "Brother Saul, the Lord Jesus, who appeared to you on the road as you came, has sent me that you may receive your sight and be filled with the Holy Spirit" (Acts 9:17 NKJV). Immediately Saul could see, arose, and was baptized.

God will sometimes give you instructions that you will hesitate to obey. You may wonder if it's actually God you're hearing or just your own imagination—or worse yet, the voice of the enemy. And frankly, we frequently mistake our own thoughts and impulses as God's voice. But Ananias *knew* he was hearing from God and called Him "Lord."

This story also demonstrates that God is able to guide His children with amazing accuracy. He not only told

Ananias where to find Saul, but revealed to Saul the name of the man who was about to come and heal him. You may wish that God would speak to you as clearly and in such detail, but most of the time we must be satisfied with general indications.

But rest assured that even if you have difficulty hearing from God, He has no problem hearing you. So even if you're often frustrated with your inability to discern God's leading and guidance clearly, you should still pray. He can make your path very obvious.

94. Prayers Rising as a Memorial

At Caesarea there was a Roman soldier named Cornelius, a centurion in the Italian Regiment. He and all his family were devout believers, and he gave generously to those in need and prayed to God regularly. One day at about 3:00 p.m. he had a vision. An angel of God in shining clothing appeared to him and announced, "Cornelius!"

Cornelius stared at him wide-eyed and asked, "What is it, Lord?"

The angel replied, "Your prayers and gifts to the poor have come up as a memorial offering before God. Now send men to Joppa to bring back a man named Simon who is called Peter. He is staying with Simon the tanner, whose house is by the sea. . . . He will bring you a message through which you and all your household will be saved" (Acts 10:3–6; 11:14 NIV).

After the angel vanished, Cornelius called two of his servants and a devout soldier. He told them what had happened and sent them to Joppa to find Peter.

When describing the incident later, Cornelius said the angel had told him, "God has heard your prayer and remembered your gifts to the poor" (Acts 10:31 NIV). The angel's exact words, however, were, "Your prayers and gifts to the poor have come up *as a memorial offering* before God (emphasis added)." Cornelius had prayed regularly, but he probably had little indication that many of his prayers had been heard. But at the *right* time, God acknowledged and answered him.

The book of Revelation says: "Another angel. . .was given much incense to offer, with the prayers of all God's people, on the golden altar in front of the throne. The smoke of the incense, together with the prayers of God's people, went up before God from the angel's hand" (Revelation 8:3–4 NIV).

In the Old Testament, a memorial offering was a handful of fine flour and oil with frankincense. The priest burned it "as a memorial on the altar, an offering made by fire, a sweet aroma to the LORD" (Leviticus 2:2 NKJV). You may pray for something often and think your prayers go unheard, but the opposite is true: they arise as a sweet aroma to God. There is a set time for God to answer, and in due season He will answer.

95. Saying No to God

Cornelius sent three men to Joppa, and they arrived the next day at noon. Meanwhile, Peter went up on the flat roof of Simon's house to pray. He was hungry, and while a meal was being prepared, he fell into a trance. He saw the heavens open, and a large sheet was let down. In the sheet were all kinds of strange animals, reptiles, and birds.

Then a voice said, "Get up, Peter; kill and eat them" (Acts 10:13 NLT).

Astonished, Peter argued, "No, Lord. . .I have never eaten anything that our Jewish laws have declared impure and unclean" (Acts 10:14 NLT).

"But the voice spoke again: 'Do not call something unclean if God has made it clean' " (Acts 10:15 NLT).

The vision was repeated three times; then the sheet was pulled up to heaven. Just then the Romans arrived, and the Holy Spirit told Peter to go with them without hesitation. So the next day he accompanied them to Caesarea. Once there, he told Cornelius and the assembled Romans, "You know it is against our laws for a Jewish man to enter a Gentile home like this or to associate with you. But God has shown me that I should no longer think of anyone as impure or unclean" (Acts 10:28 NLT).

Some Christians teach that this vision meant that unclean foods (such as pork and seafood) forbidden in Leviticus 11 were now approved for eating, but while that is an interpretation, the main, clear meaning is that the kingdom of God was now open to Gentiles.

This story also demonstrates how not to pray. Peter said, "No, Lord"—but to acknowledge God as Lord is to acknowledge Him as Master. You don't tell your master no. Like

Saul, you ask, "What shall I do, Lord?" Yet how often do we refuse God's direction?

Some Christians think they have the authority, when they pray, to command God, and cite this verse: "Thus saith the LORD. . .concerning the work of my hands command ye me" (Isaiah 45:11 KJV). But the NIV reads: "This is what the LORD says. . .do you. . .give me orders about the work of my hands?" Isaiah 45:9 clarifies whom God was talking to: "Woe to those who quarrel with their Maker (NIV)." They *try* to command God but are in no position to do so.

96. The Ephesian Benediction

Paul prayed a powerful prayer for the Ephesian Christians. It is perhaps the most beautiful benediction in the New Testament:

"For this reason I bow my knees before the Father, from whom every family in heaven and on earth derives its name, that He would grant you, according to the riches of His glory, to be strengthened with power through His Spirit in the inner man, so that Christ may dwell in your hearts through faith; and that you, being rooted and grounded in love, may be able to comprehend with all the saints what is the breadth and length and height and depth, and to know the love of Christ which surpasses knowledge, that you may be filled up to all the fullness of God. Now to Him who is able to do far more abundantly beyond all that we ask or think, according to the power that works within us, to Him be the glory in the church and in Christ Jesus to all generations forever and ever. Amen" (Ephesians 3:14–21 NASB).

Paul prayed "that Christ may dwell in your hearts through faith." This is the most vital prayer. When people have faith in Christ, God sends the Spirit of His Son into their hearts (Galatians 4:6).

Paul prayed "that you [may be] rooted and grounded in love." Faith without love is sterile. "When we place our faith in Christ Jesus. . .what is important is faith expressing itself in love" (Galatians 5:6 NLT). This fulfills the two greatest commandments—to love God and your fellow man (Matthew 22:36–40).

Paul asked "that He would grant you. . .to be strengthened with power through His Spirit in the inner man." Jesus promised, "You will receive power when the Holy Spirit comes on you" (Acts 1:8 NIV), and you must continually yield to the Spirit (Acts 5:32).

Then Paul prayed that you may "know the love of Christ which surpasses knowledge." You must never forget how much Jesus loves you. This will cause you to love and serve Him. "We love him, because he first loved us" (1 John 4:19 KJV).

Finally, Paul asked "that you may be filled up to all the fullness of God." So you will "become mature, attaining to the whole measure of the fullness of Christ" (Ephesians 4:13 NIV).

97. Paul's Prayers for the Churches

The Bible gives a clear picture of Paul's daily prayers for the churches. It might surprise you to learn that he didn't pray that they'd grow in numbers, evangelize the lost better, avoid persecution, or be blessed financially. He wrote to the believers in Philippi: "In all my prayers for all of you, I always pray with joy. . . . And this is my prayer: that your love may abound more and more in knowledge and depth of insight, so that you may be able to discern what is best and may be pure and blameless for the day of Christ, filled with the fruit of righteousness" (Philippians 1:4, 9–11 NIV).

To the believers in Colosse, Paul wrote: "We continually ask God to fill you with the knowledge of his will. . .so that you may live a life worthy of the Lord and please him in every way: bearing fruit in every good work, growing in the knowledge of God, being strengthened. . .so that you may have great endurance and patience, and giving joyful thanks to the Father" (Colossians 1:9–12 NIV).

Paul encouraged the church in Ephesus: "I keep asking that [God] may give you the Spirit of wisdom and revelation, so that you may know him better. I pray that the eyes of your heart may be enlightened in order that you may know the hope to which he has called you" (Ephesians 1:17–18 NIV).

It's important to pray for finances, evangelism, and increase, but all these are a natural outgrowth of believers' most *basic* needs—to walk in the love and knowledge of Christ. These passages inspire prayer for yourself, for your loved ones, and for your church.

Paul asked for them to love more, know Christ better, be pure and blameless and filled with righteousness and knowledge of God's will. His desire was that they have endurance and patience and joyfully thank God so that they could live lives worthy of the Lord.

98. Praising God in Heaven

Heaven is filled with the presence and glory of God, and all living beings—from angels to saints to exalted elders to great beasts—praise Him.

The four beasts around the throne say, "Holy, holy, holy, Lord God Almighty, who was and is and is to come!" Whenever they give glory and honor and thanks to Him who sits on the throne, the twenty-four elders fall down and worship Him, saying: "You are worthy, O Lord, to receive glory and honor and power; for You created all things, and by Your will they exist and were created" (Revelation 4:8–11 NKJV).

The elders sing a new song to Jesus: "You are worthy. . .for You were slain, and have redeemed us to God by Your blood out of every tribe and tongue and people and nation, and have made us kings and priests to our God; and we shall reign on the earth" (Revelation 5:9–10 NKJV).

The angels and all the creatures in heaven sing: "Worthy is the Lamb who was slaughtered—to receive power and riches and wisdom and strength and honor and glory and blessing." Then all creatures—in heaven, on and under earth, and in the sea—sing, "Blessing and honor and glory and power belong to the one sitting on the throne and to the Lamb forever and ever" (Revelation 5:12–13 NLT).

The Bible doesn't talk much about saints petitioning God in heaven. That's because "there will be no more death or mourning or crying or pain" (Revelation 21:4 NIV). There will be no problems or lack in heaven, so you won't need to pray for relief from these things. But the Bible talks a great deal about saints praising God in heaven—one of the highest forms of prayer.

Some people have the mistaken idea that that's *all* we will do in heaven, *ever*. But though believers will certainly spend time basking in the presence of God, there will also be many other fascinating, exciting activities. And you don't need to be standing before His throne to commune with Him. His presence and glory fill the entire heavenly city, and you can speak to Him and hear from Him all the time.

99. Prayers for Vengeance in Heaven

When John was in heaven, he "saw under the altar the souls of those who had been slain because of the word of God and the testimony they had maintained. They called out in a loud voice, 'How long, Sovereign Lord, holy and true, until you judge the inhabitants of the earth and avenge our blood?' Then each of them was given a white robe, and they were told to wait a little longer, until the full number of their fellow servants. . .were killed just as they had been" (Revelation 6:9–11 NIV).

Some Christians think that the martyrs should have simply forgiven their killers, not prayed for vengeance. But while believers are asked to forgive their persecutors in the here and now, God will eventually judge them. Paul said, "It is a righteous thing with God to repay with tribulation those who trouble you . . .when the Lord Jesus is revealed from heaven with His mighty angels, in flaming fire taking vengeance" (2 Thessalonians 1:6–8 NKJV). When Jesus comes from heaven with the angels, Judgment Day arrives (Matthew 25:31–33).

God *is* the avenger of the weak, and under the law of Moses, God meted out vengeance in this life. He warned, "If you afflict them in any way, and they cry *at all* to Me, I will surely hear their cry; and My wrath will become hot" (Exodus 22:23–24 NKJV, emphasis added). But if the victim follows the teachings of Jesus instead and forgives, God can show mercy to the offender. . .in this life.

If the offender *still* doesn't repent after all the generous love and mercy shown to him, his judgment will be even worse in the hereafter. "Dearly beloved, avenge not yourselves, but rather give place unto wrath: for it is written, Vengeance is mine; I will repay, saith the Lord" (Romans 12:19 KJV). The Bible then warns, "If your enemy is hungry, feed him; if he is thirsty, give him a drink; for in so doing you will heap coals of fire on his head" (Romans 12:20 NKJV).

There is a set time for God's judgment, as the martyrs found out. You may not be pleased to hear that you need to "wait a little longer" for some unbearable situation to be resolved, but that's often what God requires.

100. In Jesus' Name, Amen

John wrote, "I looked, and behold, a great multitude which no one could number, of all nations, tribes, peoples, and tongues, standing before the throne and before the Lamb. . .crying out with a loud voice, saying, 'Salvation belongs to our God who sits on the throne, and to the Lamb!' All the angels stood around the throne and the elders and the four living creatures, and fell on their faces before the throne and worshiped God, saying: 'Amen! Blessing and glory and wisdom, thanksgiving and honor and power and might, be to our God forever and ever. Amen' " (Revelation 7:9–12 NKJV).

The angels started and ended their praise with "Amen!" In the first instance, they were saying "Amen!" to the saints' exclamation of praise, stating their agreement with it. Believers habitually say, "Amen" at the end of their prayers, and it literally means, "So be it!"—in other words, "Let it be just as I prayed!"

Just before He departed for heaven, Jesus told His disciples, "Until now you have asked nothing in My name. Ask, and you will receive" (John 16:24 NKJV). So for two thousand years, we have ended our prayers with, "In Jesus' name, amen." Many people aren't sure *why* this is required, but they know that Jesus promised: "If you ask anything in My name, I will do it," and "Whatever you ask the Father in My name He will give you" (John 14:14; 16:23 NKJV).

When you make requests in Jesus' name, if you're submitted to *His* will, asking for things *He* wants you to have, it's as if Jesus Himself is asking His Father. Jesus' name is on the request form. And the Father won't refuse His Son. As Jesus explained, "All that belongs to the Father is mine" (John 16:15 NLT).

When Ezra went to Judah, he carried an official letter from

King Artaxerxes in which the king commanded his treasurers to provide whatever he might ask them (Ezra 7:21). Just so, there's power in making requests in Jesus' name, in coming "in the name of the King," but only if you're asking for things within His will.

If we would pray with a greater awareness of the power of Jesus' name, and of the meaning of the simple word *Amen*, more of our prayers would be answered.